GROWING UP GRONK

The Gronkowski boys exhibited a love of sports from an early age. Top, from left, Dan, Chris, and Gordie. Seated, from left, Rob and Goose.

GROWING UP
GRONK

A FAMILY'S STORY OF RAISING CHAMPIONS

The Gronkowski Family
with Jeff Schober

HOUGHTON MIFFLIN HARCOURT

BOSTON   NEW YORK   2013

Copyright © 2013 by The Gronkowski Family with Jeff Schober

All rights reserved

For information about permission to reproduce selections from this book,
write to Permissions, Houghton Mifflin Harcourt Publishing Company,
215 Park Avenue South, New York, New York 10003.

www.hmhbooks.com

Library of Congress Cataloging-in-Publication Data is available.
ISBN 978-0-544-12668-8

Printed in the United States of America
DOC 10 9 8 7 6 5 4 3 2 1

Contents

GRONK LINEUP   vii

INTRODUCTION: THE DAY THE DREAM TURNED REAL   xi

1. A Star Is Born   1
2. Gordy: Papa Gronk   11
3. The Evolution of Training   31
4. Gordie Jr.: Doesn't He Know the Rest of the Family Plays Football?   45
5. Mental Toughness   67
6. Dan: The Talented Workhorse   81
7. Competition and Physical Play   99
8. Chris: Brains and a Pedigree   115
9. A New Generation of Tight Ends   133
10. Rob: The Superstar   143
11. Rob Explodes   161
12. Goose: Greatness Expected   179
13. Get Gronked!   191

ACKNOWLEDGMENTS   201

Gronk Lineup

GORDY GRONKOWSKI

Born: July 13, 1959	6'3"/230 pounds

Father of Gordie, Dan, Chris, Rob, and Goose

West Seneca West High School, class of 1977
High school sports: football, basketball, baseball

Syracuse University, class of 1982
Degree: business major–transportation/marketing
College sport: football
Position: offensive and defensive lineman

Career:
- Former vice president of sales, Superior Oil
- Owner, G&G Fitness

GORDIE GRONKOWSKI JR.

Born: June 26, 1983	6'6"/250 pounds

Williamsville North High School, class of 2001
High school sports: golf, baseball, basketball, hockey

Jacksonville University, class of 2006
Degree: business
College sport: baseball
Position: first base

Career:
- Drafted 49th round by Los Angeles Angels, 2006
- Minor league/independent league baseball player
- Manager, The Fitness Store, seven locations in Ohio

DAN GRONKOWSKI

Born: January 21, 1985	6'6"/270 pounds

Williamsville North High School, class of 2003
High school sports: football, baseball, hockey, basketball

University of Maryland, class of 2008
Degree: marketing; master's in business
College sport: football
Position: tight end

Career:
- Drafted in 7th round by Detroit Lions in 2009, 255th overall
- Played for Detroit Lions, Denver Broncos, New England Patriots, and Cleveland Browns

CHRIS GRONKOWSKI

Born: December 26, 1986	6'2"/245 pounds

Williamsville North High School, class of 2005
High school sports: football, baseball, hockey

University of Maryland, 2005–7
University of Arizona, 2007–10
Degree: accounting
College sport: football
Position: fullback

Career:
- Signed as free agent with Dallas Cowboys, 2010
- Played for Dallas Cowboys, Indianapolis Colts, and Denver Broncos

ROB GRONKOWSKI

Born: May 14, 1989	6'6"/265 pounds

Williamsville North High School, grades nine through eleven
Woodland Hills High School, class of 2007
High school sports: football, basketball, baseball

University of Arizona, 2007-10
College sport: football
Position: tight end

Career:
- Drafted in 2nd round by New England Patriots in 2010, 42nd overall
- Set six NFL records in second pro season, 2011

GLENN (GOOSE) GRONKOWSKI

Born: March 25, 1993	6'3"/225 pounds and growing

Williamsville North High School, class of 2011
High school sports: football, baseball, basketball

Kansas State University, beginning in 2012
College sport: football
Position: H-back

Career:
- Set school records at Williamsville North High School for receptions, yards, and touchdowns

Proudly sporting Patriots caps at Rob's draft day in 2010.
From left, Gordie, Chris, Rob, Goose, and Dan.

Rob, Dan, Goose, Gordie, and Chris, 1994.

The Day the Dream Turned Real

"I have three sons playing in the NFL . . ."

— GORDY GRONKOWSKI

O N THE FIRST SATURDAY in September, 2010, Gordon Gronkowski sat unobtrusively in the top row of bleachers at Riverside Stadium in Buffalo, New York, wearing sunglasses and a New England Patriots sweatshirt. Considering his location, this was a daring fashion statement. The Patriots had beaten the hometown Bills for fifteen consecutive games, twice a year every year dating back to 2002. But Gronkowski had a good reason for donning that sweatshirt. One of his sons had just made the Pats' roster as a rookie tight end.

"Unobtrusive" is not a word normally used to describe the fifty-two-year-old Gronkowski. With a light brush cut beginning to fleck gray, he is a big man, standing six feet three inches, with a wide chest, hands the size of salad plates, and biceps like snow tires. On that afternoon, he alternately leaned forward and reclined, his back against a cyclone fence, then stood to pace, expression stoic to observers. His mind tumbled with possibilities.

It was opening day for high school football season in Western New York. On the field below, his youngest son, Glenn, nicknamed Goose, had just begun his senior year playing for Williamsville North, a suburban high school. As Gordy watched, Goose lit up the turf, catching a twenty-two-yard touchdown pass, returning an interception fifty-five yards for another score, and kicking four extra points en route to a 34–16 victory. It was a good start, another step along the way in the push toward a college scholarship. Although his name carried a pedigree, the kid still needed to perform.

Accompanying Gordy was his second son, Dan, who had driven home from Detroit to fill time during his weekend off. Sporting a backwards baseball cap and zip-up jacket, Dan checked the clock often, concealing his nerves behind sunglasses that matched his father's. At the far end of Lake Erie, the Detroit Lions' brain trust was making final cuts to shape its regular-season team. A second-year tight end, Danny lingered on the bubble. Through 2009 he had bounced between the practice squad and active roster. This summer, he had competed hard during training camp, hoping his efforts on the field would be rewarded. Still, not knowing was difficult. Sitting, waiting, watching the clock . . . Being with Dad at his little brother's game provided a temporary distraction.

A newspaper reporter wandered by, shook hands with Gordy and Dan, and asked how things were going.

Gordy smiled and said there was no news on Danny's future just yet. But he boasted about his eldest son, Gordie (who spells his name with an "ie" to distinguish himself from his dad), the one family member who had chosen to pursue a baseball career while the others thrived in football. Gordie had hit a home run for the Gateway Grizzlies of the Frontier League the day before. Twenty-seven, he had been a star at Jacksonville University and former major-league prospect before a back injury hampered his big-league dreams. Dad proudly recited the son's statistics: forty-five games, sixteen home runs, forty-nine RBIs, and a .318 batting average while playing first base and driving toward the play-offs.

"An inspiring story," Gordy nodded. "Determination has got this kid everywhere."

What about Rob and Chris?, the reporter asked. Have you heard anything from either of them?

Rob was a lock to make the New England Patriots, so long as his back injury did not flare. Through training camp so far, it had not. He'd performed well and impressed the coaches in spite of his youth. The fourth son, twenty-one, Rob had played tight end for two years at the University of Arizona before back surgery wiped out his junior year. Once recovered, he chose to forgo his senior season and leap into the National Football League draft, where the Patriots selected him in the second round, forty-second overall. Rob had speed, blocking ability, and size enough to provide a big target in the end zone for quarterback Tom Brady.

Gordy wasn't worried about Rob's chances. But Chris and Danny . . .

He checked his phone. No new updates. No text messages.

Chris, the middle son, was biting his nails in Dallas, waiting to learn his fate with the Cowboys. Chris had played two years of football at the University of Maryland before transferring to Arizona and finishing his college career, displaying enough brains and athleticism to make the NFL. But he was a fullback, a position that was becoming obsolete. Gone from Texas were the days of Daryl Johnston plowing a hole for a star running back like Emmitt Smith. Now tight ends were employed in an H-back formation. Not many teams kept a pure fullback on the roster. The odds of making the roster were long.

While Gordy paced and fretted, pondering his sons' futures, he had no idea that fringe players from the Cowboys' training camp were being herded into an office in Dallas. Names were called, and men split into two groups. One went through the near door, while others stayed seated. When the list had been recited, those remaining were congratulated for making the roster. After being handed a playbook, they were instructed to prepare for the season opener in eight days.

At 2:00 P.M., Chris texted his father the good news.

Gordy's chest swelled with pride. Two of his boys would play in the NFL. But he couldn't celebrate yet, not with Danny's uncertain fate.

Gordy leaned forward and whispered to the son sitting on the bench below him. "You're going to make it somewhere," he said, as much to soothe his own nerves as Danny's. "So what if the Lions bump you to their practice squad? You've been there before. If that happens, you'll get picked up by another team. The Jets need a tight end. So do the Bills."

Dan nodded, not saying anything, eyes trained on Goose's game. What was there to do but wait? One way or another, he would know by 4:00 P.M., the mandated deadline for final rosters.

Near three-thirty, Dan's phone rang. Gordy clenched his jaw, watching his son answer the call. Dan didn't talk much, but listened. A mixture of surprise and excitement crossed his face. He hung up, then turned around and looked at his dad.

"The Lions knew I wouldn't clear waivers," he said. "So I've been traded to Denver. I'm signing with the Broncos."

Gordy exhaled, patting Danny's shoulder. His son had made it. But the Broncos? That caught him off-guard. No one had expected Denver. They began to talk about logistics, flights to the Mile High City, renting a moving van and transporting everything farther west.

In the three hours that Gordy sat in Riverside Stadium watching a high school football game, his sons' futures had solidified.

Later, after the excitement died down and hours stretched toward evening, Gordy sat at his kitchen table, recognizing the day for what it was. All five of his boys were athletes, all of them great kids, and he was a proud father. Strangers had approached him over the years, watching his family succeed at sports.

"Good genes," he was told, or "lucky breaks." Gordy, however, knew the effort expended, the physical and mental commitment needed to succeed at an elite level.

"You're good," he had told the boys as they grew up. "But so are lots of other people. What's going to take you to the next level is training and commitment."

Exact numbers are difficult to find, but recent estimates are that 4.8 million children between six and thirteen play organized football in the United States. In 2009–10, the National Collegiate Athletic Association (NCAA) reported 65,648 Division I college football players. The number expands when other divisions are considered. Each NFL team carries a fifty-three-man roster, with more included on injured reserve and practice squads. Statistics show that with each higher level of play, the number of competitors sharply decreases.

That night, Gordy did not comprehend the odds, was not aware that it had been eighteen years—almost a full generation—since three brothers had played in the NFL at the same time. Then it was the Baldinger brothers, Gary, Rich, and Brian.

ESPN.com would later calculate the Gronkowski brothers' odds at one in thirty-one million. A person had a better statistical chance of winning the lottery than seeing three members of the same family play professional football. But Gordy was aware of none of that. All he knew was that their hard work was being rewarded.

He looked down at his Patriots sweatshirt. Now, he thought, I'll have to get matching ones that read "Cowboys" and "Broncos."

"Unbelievable," he said to himself. "Three of my sons are playing in the NFL."

Rob visits his former high school gym while preparing
for a photo shoot in 2012.   *Photo by Jeff Schober*

Gordy, Diane, the boys, and a giant yard stork welcome baby Rob
to the family home, 1989.

1

A Star Is Born

Gronked: To throw something down to the ground with great force, like football player Rob Gronkowski does after each touchdown. *After I finished my exam, I Gronked my pencil in a show of exuberance.*

— URBAN DICTIONARY

I N SEPTEMBER 2009, twenty-year-old Rob Gronkowski lay in bed, eyes directed at the sterile hospital ceiling. Just out of surgery, he felt like an anchor was strapped to his back. Movements were limited and tentative. A sudden shift drew sharp daggers raking against his spine. Pain had never been something he feared. Growing up in a house with four brothers, physical contact was a daily routine. As the starting tight end at the University of Arizona, he had both received and delivered major hits over the years. But this moment, coming out of surgery, was one of the most uncertain in his life.

There were legitimate questions about whether he would ever play football again. Rob never let those fears take root. Doctors had been optimistic, but there were no guarantees. And if not football, then what would he do?

The sport had defined Rob's life. His father had been a college football player who briefly played in the United States Football League (USFL) in the early 1980s. His other brother Dan, a fellow tight end, had been drafted by the Detroit Lions, while another brother, Chris, transferred from the University of Maryland after two years to play fullback alongside Rob at Arizona. The sport ran through the family's veins.

Even at a young age, Rob displayed freakish size and physical talent. He ended his senior year of high school as a six feet six SuperPrep All-American, developing blocking skills to complement eight receptions for 152 yards and four touchdowns. College-scholarship offers flooded his mailbox. In two years at Arizona, he set the school's single-game, single-season, and career records as a tight end for receptions, yards, and touchdowns.

His personality was goofy, fun-loving. It was rare to see the big boy angry or depressed. He went through each day with a smile on his face, eager to be on the field where he could line up and hit someone. There was one dream, one goal, and he had been groomed for it since he was just a little kid. Rob planned to star in the NFL.

It couldn't possibly be over, could it?

"Robbie hurt his back in the weight room doing a dead lift," his father Gordy explained. "It was the off-season after his sophomore year in college. He knew he was hurt, but thought it was just a sore back. He kept working out and running routes but was getting slower."

Back issues were not without precedent in the Gronkowski family. Rob's oldest brother, Gordie, an All-American baseball player, had suffered a herniated disk a few years earlier when in college. Once a promising major-league prospect, his injuries caused many teams to reconsider selecting him in the draft. The second brother, Dan, experienced occasional back spasms.

"I was definitely scared," Rob recalled. "Pain started in April and kept getting worse and worse. I didn't know what was going on, but I kept grinding harder because the harder you went, you didn't feel the pain for that hour. Eventually, one day, it cut off my whole nervous system going into my legs. I couldn't jump more than three inches. I kept going, but it was half-speed. I got it checked out and doctors discovered bulging and herniated disks."

Having watched one son's career veer off course because of this, Gordy wanted to be sure his other boys were protected. He had planned ahead for such a contingency.

"I took out a four-million-dollar insurance policy on Rob," Gordy said. "The insurance company believed Rob had value because he was projected to be a first- or second-round NFL draft pick. I tried to get a policy for Chris, but I couldn't. The company didn't believe he had value."

Rob's injury occurred in the L5 vertebra, located in the lower back between the hips. In addition, an MRI revealed a closing of the spinal chamber. When Rob did not work out, the affected area settled and did not bother him. But how could a football player have a career in which he didn't work out?

"Some doctors told us he shouldn't play," Gordy said. "Others said if the swelling goes down, he should be OK. And Rob at first tried to bluff and say he was fine before the surgery. But it reached a point where I could tell he was hurting, so I shut him down. He was done playing college football until this got fixed. I wasn't making many friends in Arizona, but this is my kid, you know?"

No one was quite sure how to proceed, because when Rob relaxed and did not work out, the pain lessened. The injury was not debilitating. If Rob stopped training and playing football, he could live a comfortable life. But the professional opinion was that eventually, as he aged, Rob would need surgery to repair the spine.

Gordy searched for the best back specialist around. One name kept recurring: Robert Watkins, a doctor from California who'd performed surgery on athletes with injuries similar to Rob's. The doctor laid out options.

"We went around and around about Rob's surgery," Gordy said. "He had choices. One was to not have surgery and never play football again but get four million dollars. The other was don't collect the money but have surgery and hope that everything comes out right. It wasn't an easy choice. It's a serious operation. One slip down there and you're dealing with the vertebrae and spinal cord."

The insurance policy was both a blessing and a curse. If Rob elected to walk away from football, he would be financially set for life at only twenty years old. Even though he had played only two years of college football and sat out his junior year because of the injury, Rob was talented enough that the NFL was still interested. Could he forgo his junior year of college and make a leap to the pros despite surgery?

"Four million dollars is a lot of money," Gordy mused. "With investments, I knew he could get five percent back in tax-free bonds. If he took the insurance policy, he could collect two hundred thousand tax-free every year. But if you have the operation it's like rolling the dice."

Rob ultimately made the decision: he didn't want to become wealthy from an insurance policy. He preferred to earn it. Rob agreed to back surgery, knowing it was a perilous path: his body needed to remain straight and avoid sideways moves for six weeks afterward. Recovery would be difficult, with no guarantees.

"The money was not a consideration at all," Rob said. "We were confident because of the doctor and his background. We knew he was the best. I never looked at the money option one bit. I just wanted to keep playing football, and that's what I did."

Gordy honored his son's wishes, admiring his attitude. He and his former wife had raised their boys to work hard. None expected to be handed rewards without earning them.

"I had never had surgery, never been knocked out on anesthesia before, so it was scary," Rob admitted. "For the first three days, my whole back was stiff. I wondered if I would heal, but you feel better every week. I just chilled for a month and a half, sitting on the couch. That's basically all you can do."

Bill Gorman is an assistant basketball coach at Williamsville North High School, where Rob played varsity basketball for three seasons. Like all of Rob's coaches, Gorman recognized that he was dealing with a special athlete. But more than just winning games, he was concerned about educating Rob for a life in professional sports.

"We talked about the concept that as an athlete, any success you have can be taken from you in a second because of injury," Gorman recalled. "When he told me he might not play anymore because of his back, I felt like crying. When you're in the spotlight, things are going great, and things were going great for him. I told him that now he was going to find out who his true friends were."

"He was nervous, there's no doubt," Gordy said. "But we never had a conversation about what he should do if he couldn't play football. That's not the way we think."

The insurance policy was written in such a way that Rob could proceed with surgery and play for three games to test the recovery. If the injury was not healed, he could step away from the sport and still collect the money, although he could never play again. The surgery, however, was a calculated gamble.

"This is how I looked at it at the time," Gordy recalled. "If he went back to college and the operation didn't work, he had to leave the sport before the third game. If it wasn't right in the second game, and he couldn't play, we could still get money. I believed if he made it to the NFL and got past the third game, even into the fifth or sixth before something went wrong, he'd still get a year's pay. It wouldn't have been four million, but it would have given him something."

As any football fan knows, the story turned out well. Not only did Rob get through the surgery, he was drafted by the New England Patriots in 2010 and made an immediate impact as a rookie, catching ten touchdown passes. The following season, as a twenty-two-year-old, he shattered tight end records, recording ninety receptions, 1,327 yards, and seventeen touchdowns.

Along the way, Rob became a bona fide superstar. His signature ball spike after a touchdown became known as "Gronking," a term that found its way into the Urban Dictionary. He sat for ESPN interviews. He created controversy by appearing shirtless in a photograph beside a porn star who was wearing his jersey, both of them smiling coyly. Rap singers referenced him in their lyrics. Everyone, it seemed, wanted to be near Rob Gronkowski.

To look at Rob during that season, it was hard to imagine back pain had nearly brought him to a halt two years earlier. At 265 pounds, standing at six feet six inches, Rob has a square-shaped head topped by short brown hair, his features chiseled. He resembles Ivan Drago, the Russian heavyweight from *Rocky IV,* played by a young Dolph Lundgren. His neck is muscular, shoulders wide, biceps bulging. Simply put, Rob was bigger and stronger than most everyone else.

"Rob became an overnight rock star," his father said, reflecting on the 2011 season. "I looked at the circus around him, and many times I thought, I can't believe I raised this kid."

Those who have known him for years are amused but not surprised by Rob's breakout season. His personality is lighthearted and silly, but it masks a fiercely competitive fire that was nurtured by growing up with four brothers. His ascent into the NFL record books, many believe, is simply the next step in a natural progression.

"Rob just has this fun streak about him," observed Mike Mammoliti, Rob's high school football coach during his soph-

junior years. "He was a big, happy-go-lucky kind of

kept getting bigger."

Mammoliti recalled one snapshot that embodied Rob's personality. It was opening night at Williamsville North High School's new athletic field.

"Rob was playing defensive end on the far side," Mammoliti said. "The other team's quarterback pitched the ball, and they ran a toss toward our bench. From the sideline, I saw Rob coming toward me, eyes as big as proverbial coke bottles, and he was smiling. He hit the runner and blew this kid up. He was laughing the whole time. He drove this kid two or three yards from the sideline all the way into our bench and then got up laughing. Robbie hit him while he was laughing and walked back to the huddle, laughing. I remember thinking, this kid just loves to play."

Despite his superstar status, Rob isn't the first member of his family to experience athletic success. It's doubtful he'll be the last. With a tight-knit clan of one tough dad and five tough boys, growing up Gronk has always meant being pushed and pushing back, fighting and scrapping, showing off to gain bragging rights without letting their egos become inflated.

Considering all they have experienced, the results are impressive.

The story goes back to the 1970s, long before Gordy, the patriarch, had earned the nickname Papa Gronk.

Gordy as a college football player.

Five sons cluster around Gordy, circa 1995.
Clockwise, from top left: Dan, Gordie, Rob, Goose, and Chris.

2

Gordy: Papa Gronk

"This kid's got the biggest heart of anyone I coach . . ."

— FRANK VIGGATO, HIGH SCHOOL BASEBALL COACH

GORDY GRONKOWSKI IS THE patriarch of a family of professional athletes. With his former wife, Diane, he has five sons: Gordie, born in 1983; Dan, born in 1985; Chris, born near the end of 1986; Rob, born in 1989; and Glenn (Goose), born in 1993.

In addition, Gordy is the owner of G&G Fitness, a chain of fifteen stores between Buffalo and Cincinnati that sells workout equipment to individuals and professional sports teams. He played college football at Syracuse University in the 1970s and early '80s, and was briefly on the roster of the New Jersey Generals in the short-lived USFL during the 1980s.

By all accounts, he has lived success. But Gordy admits his life was on a fast track to nowhere for much of his childhood. Things turned around after his first year of high school.

"When I was in junior high, I was a punk, fighting all the

time," he recalled. "I did everything imaginable. I never played Little Loop football because I was too fat."

Gordy grew up in West Seneca, New York, a suburb south of Buffalo. Athletic achievements stretched deep into the family's roots. Gordy's grandfather, Ignatius Gronkowski, competed as a cyclist in the 1924 Olympics in France. But his father, Ignatius Jr., was a liquor salesman whose drinking problem kept him distant from his son. Gordy's mother, Irene, was a stay-at-home mother who worked at a nursing home later in life.

"There weren't many organized sports for kids in those days," Gordy said. "We'd go around the corner to Centennial Park and play pickup games constantly. We made up all these different rules for the silly games we played."

As a freshman at West Seneca West High School, Gordy's grades hovered just above failure. Because he wanted to stay active, he became a member of the football, basketball, and baseball teams. But in his mind, athletics and academics fell worlds apart. Sports were a way to pass time, far better than sitting in a boring classroom.

He never truly connected with his father.

"My dad was very talented," Gordy said. "He was a great athlete, he could sing, he earned perfect marks on his report card. But he wasn't there for me. He pissed it all away. At the same time, I do appreciate him, because he put me on this earth. My dad made my brother and I into tough guys. Not intentionally, but we should thank him for that. If we lived a different lifestyle, we might never have known the other side."

It was Gordy's older brother, Glenn, who provided inspiration.

"He was two years ahead of me, and he was a brainiac," Gordy said. "He was six eight but only weighed a hundred and fifty pounds. He was kind of nerdy, hitting the books every day. He was a junior when I was a freshman. I looked up to him."

Around that time, recruitment letters arrived in their mailbox, requesting that Glenn consider several colleges. Academic scholarships were offered, but the combination of brains and athletics opened doors. Most were Division III schools, yet they were invitations to college at a reduced rate. Gordy was impressed.

"That's when I started waking up," he said. "Was I going to act like an idiot all my life or was I going to prove myself? My dad was a heavy drinker, and I didn't want to go down that path. In the back of my head, I thought about going into the military. But my brother inspired me to come out of my shell and push myself."

"He never studied much, that's for sure," said Glenn Gronkowski, Gordy's brother. "Growing up, Gordy was a little butterball, small and chubby. When we played pickup games, he'd get pushed around, and we had to coax him to try again. But he started to work at things, and after a while, lifting weights and getting strong, he developed into a pretty good athlete. It was the same with his schoolwork. He didn't take it seriously at first, but then he picked it up as he grew older."

In a short time, Gordy matured and began to apply himself. His tenth-grade average shot up to 90 percent, a significant jump from the 65 percent of a year earlier. (When he graduated in 1977, his overall grade point average was 86. "It would have been higher if I didn't screw up that first year," he reflected.)

Meanwhile, older brother Glenn received a partial scholarship to play football at Rochester Institute of Technology, and later transferred to Canisius College when RIT dropped its football program. That inspired his younger brother, who believed he could achieve the same thing.

"Baseball was my favorite sport," Gordy said. "I always wanted to play at the next level, but I threw my arm out so I knew I wasn't going anywhere there. I decided to concentrate on football."

With Glenn off to college, Gordy made a commitment to himself: he would add strength and focus on getting bigger. Increasing size was a way to push himself, a way to demonstrate to skeptics that he possessed internal motivation, a drive to succeed.

"I was out to prove people wrong," he admitted. "I wanted to show my dad that I was somebody special."

The winter of his junior year, he elected not to play basketball, but instead hit the weight room, training daily. By his senior year, results showed on the football field. Older and stronger, he played on both sides of the ball, offensive and defensive tackle, and turned in a successful season.

"But I didn't get any letters from colleges, and I couldn't understand it," he said. "My brother had a stack of them when he was my age."

Gordy approached his football coach, Fred Lampman, asking when recruiters might reach out to him. The coach smirked, turned, and walked away. There were politics involved, and unfortunately, Lampman didn't believe Gordy was good enough to play college ball.

"I didn't know all this at the time, but the way the process works is that high school coaches get questionnaire cards from colleges at the beginning of the season asking if anyone has potential. As a coach, you don't want to put down anything that isn't true. If you say a kid is six six, three hundred pounds, and running a four-seven forty-yard dash, he'd better be doing it. If a scout from UCLA comes all the way out here to see the kid is only six three, weighs two forty, and runs a five-two forty, then that's a problem. Unfortunately, that happens, take my word. But coaches start the recruiting process through these questionnaires."

Lampman believed two other players on his team were a better fit for college football, so he pushed them instead of Gronkowski. Jim Hatter received stacks of recruitment letters and ended up playing at the University of Buffalo. The other, Dennis Hartman, ultimately played fullback at Syracuse University. No one knew it at the time, but without Hartman, Gordy's life would have taken a very different path.

"When my coach gave me the brushoff, that lit a fire in me," Gordy said. "He didn't think I was good enough. I thought, Screw you. I'll prove you wrong."

Gordy informed his baseball coach not to expect him for practice during spring break. He devised a plan to travel across the country on a Greyhound bus to the West Coast, where he scheduled interviews with football coaches. He composed introductory letters to a number of schools, including UCLA, UC Davis, Berkeley, and Long Beach State.

"My family didn't have much money, and if sports didn't work out, I looked into joining the Marines," he recalled. "But I thought I'd give it one last shot to see if I could catch on some-where in football. At the time, an open ticket for a Greyhound bus was two hundred and forty dollars. You could go anywhere. They would drop you off at a bus station in any major city. You had to show your pass when you got back on, and the ride would continue wherever you wanted."

California was a mythical paradise to Gordy's teenage senses. He had spent his youth watching UCLA and the University of Southern California play in the Rose Bowl. The image of sun-shine and surfboards was another lure. Mostly, though, he wanted to travel somewhere new, where he could escape the doubting eyes of his father and his coaches.

Accompanied by a classmate, Guy Bryant, Gordy packed a white Adidas bag with enough clothes for a weeklong trip. Be-fore they left home, he conducted reconnaissance on the coach's office, ducking inside when the coast was clear.

"I stole the canisters that had our game films," Gordy admit-ted with a smile. "They were eight-millimeter. The quality was terrible. But my coach wouldn't give them to me, and I needed them if I was going to convince a football program to let me into college."

Guy Bryant remains friends with Gordy nearly thirty-five years later.

"We were two eighteen-year-old kids who had just come through the winter of 1977, which was one of the worst in Buf-falo history," Bryant recalled. "I was interested in going to school in California, so I joined Gordy. Originally, we planned to drive Gordy's car, but when his father wouldn't pay the insurance, we took a bus for sixty-four hours. We saw the armpit of every city from here to the Pacific Ocean."

Carrying those films into a series of West Coast offices, Gordy had varying degrees of success. UC Davis was Division II, and team officials suggested there would be no problem adding him to their football program. But Davis did not have a business track, and Gordy wanted to study business. Coaches at Berkeley were uninterested. UCLA suggested Gordy attend Bakersfield, a junior college, to prove his football skills there. While this wouldn't have been his first choice, at that point Gordy was thrilled to have a legitimate chance to attend college.

But the next visit, Long Beach State, offered a better option.

"I bonded with their guy right away," Gordy recalled. "He took my film, left me sitting there, and went into a room to watch it."

When the coach emerged a while later, he smiled at Gordy.

"I like what I just saw," he said, handing the canisters back. "We always hold out one scholarship for kids who didn't get recruited, kids like you." He paused. "Do you want to come to Long Beach?"

Gordy felt like he was walking on air. The coach did not know that to save on hotel expenses, he and Guy had been sleeping on a bus moving up and down the coast.

"Some stories from that trip still can't be told," Guy joked. "Gordy got a horrible sunburn one day. Overall, California was a pretty liberal place compared to Buffalo. We saw a different side of the world."

After a quick visit to San Diego State — the coaches liked him but were out of scholarships — Gordy returned home, where he was met with disbelief that his aggressive approach had been successful.

"People couldn't believe that I got a full ride to Long Beach State," he said. "My father told me I was nuts. But my baseball coach, Frank Viggato, was a big supporter. He thought my West Coast trip was the greatest thing. In fact, he was in the athletic office at West Seneca West when Long Beach State called, asking to speak with my football coach. Knowing the relationship between me and Fred Lampman wasn't so great, Viggato took the call and said there was no need to talk to anyone besides him."

The plan to enlist in the Marines was jettisoned. Instead, Gordy prepared for a move to California after graduating from high school in 1977. But a varsity baseball game that spring altered the direction of Gordy's life.

Jerry Angelo was the defensive tackle coach at Syracuse University. (By 2011, he had moved up the football ladder to become general manager of the Chicago Bears.) Angelo had recruited Gordy's classmate, Dennis Hartman, to play football for the Orange. One afternoon, as Angelo was driving through Western New York, he stopped to see his star recruit playing high school baseball. Hartman was big, an impressive power hitter, but another kid caught Angelo's eye.

"I was smacking the ball over the center-field fence during warm-ups," Gordy recalled, "and I went on to have a pretty good game."

During the game, Angelo approached Viggato, the baseball coach.

"Who is that?" he asked, pointing.

"Gordy Gronkowski." Viggato did not hesitate. "I love the kid and he's getting screwed. He's got the biggest heart of anyone I coach. For a while it didn't look like he was going to be playing football anymore. But let me tell you how he just landed a scholarship to Long Beach State . . ."

Angelo was intrigued. When the game ended, he introduced himself to Gordy, asking if his football coach would loan him film of Gordy playing. Gordy was quick to jump on the idea.

"I can save you the hassle of talking to my coaches," he said. "The game films are in the backseat of my car."

No promises were made, but Angelo took the metal canisters and drove back to Syracuse. A few days later, Gordy received a call asking him to visit the campus, where he would interview with Frank Maloney, the head coach.

"I had just taken a cross-country trip, but that was riding a bus," Gordy said. "I had never driven outside of Buffalo before. I got in my car and drove to Syracuse. I was a little lighter that spring because of baseball, so the whole time before I got to campus I was eating canisters of mashed potatoes, trying to add weight. Someone had told me that instant potatoes would add five or ten pounds to you if you ate enough."

He tipped the scale at 230, considered a decent size for a defensive tackle at the time. Gordy spoke with the young head coach for longer than expected and was finally offered the program's final scholarship.

"I've always thought about how many things had to line up for my life to go in that direction," Gordy reflected. "I was recruited by accident because of Dennis Hartman. Jerry Angelo was coming through the area and just decided to stop and see one of his prospects. It was a freak thing that I happened to be in the right place at the right time. What if Angelo had just driven home instead of stopping at our game? What would have happened if I had gone to California?"

The college newspaper, the *Daily Orange*, later ran an article about Gordy under the headline "The Man Who Was Recruited with a Baseball Bat."

"My freshman year at Syracuse was great," Gordy said. "I played as a defensive tackle and as an extra lineman in short-yardage situations."

Although he did see significant playing time, Gordy was a relative unknown when he stepped onto campus. He was not a household name, nor a highly recruited prospect. Because he had signed with the program late, newspapers in Buffalo were not aware of the fact that he landed at a major football program. Gordy didn't care. His $6,500 scholarship covered everything from room and board to books and tuition. Football had opened doors.

On his first play as a college athlete, Gordy lined up against the Penn State offense. Matt Suhey, who later starred with the Chicago Bears, tried to squirt through the line. Gordy stuffed him. Filled to capacity, Archbold Stadium erupted in cheers. The loudspeaker boomed, "Tackle on Suhey made by Gronkowski." Gordy stood with his chest puffed out.

"It was a fantastic moment," he recalled. "That was when I realized how cool it was to have made it."

The next play was a repeat of the first. Again, Gordy jammed the ball carrier at the line of scrimmage. Plans for the Marines and Long Beach State were now a distant memory. "This is almost too easy," he thought.

In a short time, however, his health became an issue. He aggravated an old knee injury. For a while, he played through the pain, but calcium deposits kept growing larger until it was too difficult to run. Unable to compete in spring practices, Gordy sat out his sophomore year. Determination won him a roster spot again his junior year, but he soon contracted mono and lost thirty pounds. Much of that season was washed out as well.

Finally healthy by his senior year, Gordy switched to offensive line. Before the knee trouble flared, his forty-yard-dash times had hovered around 4.9 seconds. Afterward, he had slowed to 5.1, so coaches thought he would perform better on the other side of the ball, where blocking was more important than raw speed. The new position suited him, and Gordy had a successful year.

Because he had not played as a sophomore, Gordy was eligible for another season, and he was excited to finish his collegiate career on a high note. But a number of events conspired to make his fifth year a challenge.

"When I was getting ready for my redshirt year, I was in the weight room benching 405," Gordy said. "On my third rep I pulled my pec right off the shoulder. The team didn't even list me on the depth chart after that because they thought I was done. But I worked my butt off and got back."

Despite hours of rehab, he was now off the radar of Dick MacPherson, Syracuse's new coach, because MacPherson had not seen Gordy participate at spring workouts. Although he stood on the sidelines for his first game back, Gordy was added to special teams after that. Shortly, he was playing guard in a rotation. But the offensive-line position came with a unique role: MacPherson used guards to relay plays from the sidelines to the quarterback in the huddle.

When the season ended, Gordy was proud of his accomplishments over five years. But he wondered what his football career might have been had he remained healthy. Looking back three decades later, he is at peace with the twists of fate.

"It all worked out," Gordy recalled.

In 1982, with a college degree in hand, he wondered about the future. Was professional football an option? The NFL seemed a distant dream, but this was a young man who had scrapped and fought for everything. He recalled when his high school coach had written him off, how he bussed across the country hustling for a scholarship, then ended up playing for a college powerhouse. "Let's give it one more try," he thought.

Several upstart businessmen had begun the USFL in an attempt to rival the NFL. Promises were made to up-and-coming athletes, and several high-profile players were lured away from the NFL by big contracts.

"In their first year, I had a tryout with the New Jersey Generals," Gordy said. Former Cleveland Browns star Brian Sipe, leader of the "Cardiac Kids," was the team's quarterback. "I traveled down to New Jersey a couple times. The training lasted a few months, but once camp started, I was released. I never stepped on the field for a game."

Back in Buffalo, for a short time Gordy worked as a repo man, repossessing appliances for a rental company. Still fit from football, his weight hovering between 270 and 280 pounds, he was intimidating in the role, taking back washing machines and refrigerators from customers who could not pay. But the job was a stopgap until something better came along.

The Hamilton Tiger-Cats in the Canadian Football League offered Gordy $18,000 to play there. He turned down the offer. In addition to low pay, an unfavorable exchange rate made playing in the CFL a financial disaster. With reluctance, Gordy realized his football career was over.

"I was banged up at the time," he said. "I had already endured three surgeries, and I wasn't even twenty-five. I had trouble with my shoulder, my knee, and my ankle. Football takes a toll on your body. Years later, I always told my kids, 'If you can get through college healthy, you'll have a great shot at the pros.' But it's difficult to stay healthy."

Western New York's economy was bleak in the early 1980s. Steel plants closed and the nation was locked in a deep recession. A connection through Syracuse University helped Gordy land a job with Pennzoil in Connecticut. After a year away from Buffalo, his young wife, Diane, felt homesick, so the couple returned to Western New York, where Gordy hoped to put his business training to use. He landed at Superior, an oil company in North Tonawanda, becoming vice president of sales. It was that job that provided a springboard into owning his own company.

"I love to work out," Gordy said. "As part of my job at Superior, I went to a hotel in Buffalo for a conference and saw a machine in the weight room that was an impressive piece of equipment. It was solid and well built, not rickety. I used it and it was great."

Exercise equipment is sometimes constructed cheaply to keep the price down. But for a big man like Gordy, quality is a requirement or the machine will have a short life.

Gordy remembered the brand name, Paramount, and visited a fitness-equipment sales outlet in North Buffalo. In the mid-1980s, this was the only store of its kind in the area.

"The guy I talked to smelled like a pack of cigarettes," Gordy said with a scowl. "I mentioned Paramount but he didn't know what I was talking about."

Undaunted, he tracked down the company and phoned Paramount himself, hoping to make a purchase. But Paramount did not deal directly with customers. It only sold through distributors. There were two in the Northeast: one in Pittsburgh and the other in Asbury Park, New Jersey. During a visit to Syracuse, Gordy decided to extend his trip into Asbury Park.

"I went to a store called Fitness Lifestyles and got talking with the owner, Leo Clark," he said. Clark instantly bonded with Gordy, and more than twenty years later, they remain close friends. "His business was a high-end store with good-quality equipment for people who really care about fitness. The equipment could hold a big guy like me. That crap that gets sold in department stores isn't reliable. You step on one of their treadmills and before you know it, it's broken."

The conversation triggered Gordy's business instincts. Could a store like Fitness Lifestyles work in Buffalo?

"My brother and I traveled to Pittsburgh to watch Syracuse play a game against Pitt, and we visited a specialty fitness store down there," Gordy said. "I came away even more impressed. That's when Glenn decided he wanted to join in my venture."

Glenn admitted that the idea to develop a fitness store in Western New York was Gordy's vision. But this was not the brothers' first foray into starting a business.

"We fooled around with a couple ideas," Glenn said. "We looked into vending machines, but concluded there wasn't a steady market for that. We realized that the guy on Hertel Avenue was the only one in the area selling weights, and it was the north side of Buffalo. There was an entire market outside of the city. I had a little more free time in my job, so I was able to do things to get our store up and running."

In the fall of 1990, Gordy and Glenn christened their new business G&G Fitness. They rented a building on Transit Road in the town of Amherst. Both kept their day jobs: Gordy at Superior; Glenn at a company that manufactures products for heavy vehicles. More than twenty years later, Glenn remains a district sales·manager there.

The early days were exciting but scary. Neither brother knew how long their fledgling operation would last.

"Between us, we pooled all our money, which was around fifty thousand dollars," Gordy said. "That didn't buy much. We had three treadmills, two other machines, and lots of free weights, because they were a big thing back then. Our showroom didn't look anything like it does now. With so little equipment, our floor was pretty empty, so we spaced a bunch of trees and potted plants all around to fill it up. Any leftover money was spent on advertising."

On opening weekend in November, Gordy dressed in a rented Teenage Mutant Ninja Turtles costume and rode a stationary bicycle in the store's parking lot, hoping to attract passersby. Getting people to visit their showroom wasn't a problem. The place was mobbed. But by Sunday's end, despite an impressive amount of foot traffic, few sales had been made.

"Glenn and I got together Sunday night and realized we had just made the worst mistake in our lives," Gordy said. "We had even hired a manager, and now we wondered how we were going to pay him. That night, we tried to figure out ways we could get out of this business. I hardly slept."

Back at Superior on Monday, with a sense of foreboding Gordy waited until lunchtime to phone the store and check in. The manager was distracted, asking if he could call back. Things were busy, he explained. Gordy hung up and scratched his head.

When they finally connected a few hours later, Gordy learned that G&G Fitness had been bustling most of the day. Apparently, the myriad visitors from Saturday had returned to purchase weights after reconsidering over the weekend.

"We're over ten thousand dollars in sales so far today," the manager told Gordy.

Despite the brief windfall, there were long stretches of nail biting. Could a fitness supply store survive? Glenn recalls one sale in particular that came at an opportune time.

"When we opened in November, we didn't sell much of anything," he noted. "Maybe we sold a couple thousand dollars between then and Christmas. We didn't have money to pay our bills. The son of a prominent restaurant owner came in on Christmas Eve looking to buy a treadmill for his wife. He wanted a good one, not some piece of junk, and he was willing to spend money. He liked one that cost five thousand, and he paid cash on the spot. That saved the business for a while. We were off and running."

Despite the difficult days, Gordy began with a strong belief in G&G Fitness. That belief is still present, more than two decades later. He knows the business contributes something positive to his customers.

"I worked out all my life, and it's a passion of mine," he said. "When you sell oil, as I did at Superior, it's a commodity product. You're not helping people. When someone comes into my store and buys a two-thousand-dollar treadmill, I know for a fact that they're going to use it. People don't spend that kind of money and let it go to waste. So I just helped make that person's life better, because when you work out, you feel so much better about yourself. It's a great feeling. I've had people who are out of shape come back later and say they've lost significant pounds. There are so many success stories. To know that I helped make that person's life better and they're leading a more healthy lifestyle is an incredibly rewarding feeling."

But in the early 1990s, with each brother holding a different day job, the double duty began to take its toll.

"For a year, I was working sixty or seventy hours a week at Superior, then I'd come to G&G and work some more," Gordy said. "It was getting harder and harder to maintain that pace."

The tipping point came one night when Gordy nearly split his brother's head open because of a simple mistake.

"We were working long hours," Glenn said. "It was around one in the morning when Gordy and I were putting a machine together. We were twisting screws into this multipurpose set. I was assembling a seat, and he was attaching an overhead bar that weighed twenty or thirty pounds. He dropped it and I was right beneath him. It conked me pretty good."

Glenn believes that the corduroy baseball cap he was wearing at the time offered his scalp a tiny bit of protection. The bar glanced off the cap and clattered to the floor. Gordy cursed and checked on his brother.

"Let me see if you need stitches," he said.

Glenn waved him off. "I don't need any damn stitches," he spat angrily. "But I'm exhausted. I'm going home." He hopped in his car and drove away, wiping off the blood that trickled down his forehead.

"That's when I knew this wasn't working," Gordy said. "At the time, I had three little kids at home. I couldn't do this anymore. I made Glenn an offer. If he gave me a certain amount of money, he could have the business."

"I don't want the business," Glenn replied.

Both men thought about putting G&G Fitness up for sale and considered ways to break their building lease. After several days of deliberation, Gordy decided to flip the scenario.

"Someone needed to get serious with this," he said. "The business wasn't going anywhere, because we kept half-assing it. This time I offered Glenn the same amount of money I had proposed giving him. When he accepted, I took over."

Gordy explained the situation to his boss at Superior. He wanted to step back from the oil business but would stay long enough to help train his replacement. Although his hours were cut back, Gordy stayed with Superior for another six years.

Over time, G&G Fitness has shown the results of hard work.

By the end of 2011, the company had fifteen stores spread among three states, with prominent locations in Buffalo, Rochester, Syracuse, Pittsburgh, Cleveland, and Cincinnati. It had commercial accounts with fire companies and schools, from high school to college. It has also designed workout areas for professional teams in every major sport. The Sabres, Bills, and Bisons are Buffalo customers. Other examples are a soccer team in Rochester and the Pittsburgh Steelers.

"To his credit, Gordy always had a more grandiose plan than I did," Glenn said. "My idea was one store in Williamsville and maybe a second one if we had enough success. Maybe something in Rochester, or if we pushed it, Syracuse. I always thought it would be limited to the two of us and a store manager, but he took it further. The whole thing was Gordy's idea, and he ran with it. I'm really proud of my little brother's vision."

The shirtless Gronkowski boys ham it up for the camera, circa 1996.

May 2012: Rob, Chris, and Dan pose for a *Muscle and Fitness* photo shoot in the family's Amherst, New York, basement.

3

The Evolution of Training

"My goal in life was to get [my boys] to college and get
that paid for . . . Anything after that was a bonus."

— GORDY GRONKOWSKI

THE SPORTING WORLD IS a different place now than it
was in the early 1980s when Gordy played college football.
When he was released from the New Jersey Generals, he
tipped the scales at between 270 and 280 pounds.

"I was considered huge back then," Gordy said. "In 1982, there
were two three-hundred-pound guys playing in the NFL. Contrast that with today. I went through stats for 2010, and there
were a hundred and eighty-six guys over three hundred pounds
and two who weighed more than four hundred. At this rate of
change, what will things be like in another thirty years?"

During Gordy's playing days, defensive ends routinely
weighed 235, and a big nose tackle was 240. Carrying forty
pounds more than most of the men he lined up against, Gordy
seemed like a monster on the offensive line.

Many factors contributed to players getting bigger and stronger as time passed, according to Gordy.

"Nautilus equipment came into play in the early eighties," he said. "And there were steroids. People got real big real fast. The people around me who used steroids all ended up playing at the next level."

Sports fitness has come a long way in a few decades. When Gordy first began playing football at Syracuse University in 1977, the weight room contained two bench presses and little else.

"Our weight room was the size of a closet," he said. "Now, when you go to a major college, it's unbelievable the amount of equipment that's available. At the time, we didn't have a strength coach. Your football coaches were your strength coaches. It was only in my last two years of college that we got a strength coach. That's when Syracuse built a room with Nautilus machines to help improve our conditioning."

A typical training regimen three decades ago followed a simple motto: no pain, no gain. For Gordy's generation, this skewed method of thinking has created long-term and residual health effects.

"I killed my body," he said. "Getting bigger was my decision, but I went totally overboard with it. All those people who said I'd never make it, I was out to prove them wrong. Anytime I didn't want to do a workout, I thought of them and it lit a fire under me."

It was, Gordy admits now, the wrong approach to training.

"Back then, no one knew how to work out properly. I used to lift three hours a day, bench-pressing religiously. I blew out all my joints but was bigger than a brick house. It seemed worth it at the time, but looking back, it was overkill."

Because of Gordy's experience, when his sons reached the proper age to begin a fitness program, Gordy made sure they did not repeat his mistakes.

None of the Gronkowski boys played organized football until they reached eighth grade. Keeping them away from the game was a conscious decision by their father, who claims there were several factors behind that choice.

"First off, they were all too big," he recalled. "They would have had to lose a few pounds to make weight restrictions, and I didn't believe in diets at that age. Also, as a former player, I went out and talked with coaches in Little League football, and some of the coaches didn't know what they were doing. Not all of them, but the majority of coaches were there because they wanted to make sure their kid got to play."

A focus on technique or helping players improve was not evident at that level. Most of the time, the fastest kid was put in the backfield and told simply to run until he was caught.

"When my kids played baseball and hockey, I could tell they were far ahead of everyone else athletically," Gordy said. "My big dream from the start was to get them all college scholarships, so I had a bigger plan for my kids than Little League football. The reality is, I didn't want to burn them out at a young age. I didn't want them to hate the game."

Gordy admits that his approach was unique and probably would not be advisable for the parent of an average kid.

"For the normal family, playing youth football might be the only time the kid gets to play," he noted. "As a boy grows, he might be cut from his high school team, but at a young age, he's the same size as everybody else. It's different for everyone, but in that situation, playing football might be a good thing."

Gordie Jr., the oldest of the five Gronkowski brothers, was a multisport athlete at Williamsville North High School, playing basketball, baseball, and club hockey. He even lettered in golf as a ninth grader. When he was fourteen, his father approached him about beginning a regular workout schedule outside of team practices.

"One of the myths to strength and performance training is that kids are too young," said Demeris Johnson, a former NFL defensive back who trains high school athletes in Western New York. "Science tells us—and this is not me or any other professional just talking—but science tells us that the younger you start, the better. Most folks, when they think of strength training, they think heavy weights. But at six years old, kids can do core training: sit-ups, push-ups, chin-ups. I'm not saying put a six-year-old on the squat rack, but at that age he can start with core mechanics and speed."

"Kids can start training at an early age, but they have to go about it the right way," Gordy agreed. With his experience in fitness, Gordy understood how to set up a proper regimen. He didn't want to start a kid too young, because he believed that could have a negative effect on muscle growth. But when his son reached eighth grade, it was time. Gordie, however, wasn't interested.

"I didn't really know or understand how important training was or how it would affect my life," Gordie reflected, looking back many years later. "My dad didn't push me when I was younger. He gave me the option and let me go."

It wasn't until Danny, the second son, broke his ankle during a football game in eighth grade that a workout program began in the Gronkowski family. The fact that Gordy owned a fitness equipment store meant that their basement was stocked with weights and workout machines that Gordy used himself.

"This injury gives us a perfect opportunity to start working your body," Gordy preached to Danny. "Let's start the program now."

Dan agreed. It was a slow go at first, according to Gordy. Father and son met in the basement. Gordy supervised, lying down on the weight bench to demonstrate proper form. He kept his back flat on the bench, elbows close to his body, slowly raising and lowering the bar. Initially, Danny didn't have enough strength to lift an empty iron bar, let alone one with weights on each end. So he began using a broomstick to master the movement.

"An Olympic bar weighs forty-five pounds, which doesn't seem like much, but that's heavy for an eighth-grader," Gordy noted. "We started with light weights, three reps of fifteen. There were three rest days in between each muscle group. And I stressed flexibility. We stretched and then stretched some more."

Gordy taped a colored poster to the wall showing the human body and its different muscle groups. He taught his son that each exercise targeted a different muscle group, teaching about biceps, triceps, and quads.

Once his technique was mastered, Dan gained strength in a

short period of time. Gordie, by then a high school sophomore, noticed the change, second-guessing his decision to avoid workouts. Suddenly he wanted to train, too.

"Danny was getting bigger and looking great," Gordie recalled. "He was quicker and more athletic, and that made me think that maybe I needed to try this out. Even though he was two years younger than me, in a short time he was playing on all my varsity teams in high school."

Much like Gordy tried to emulate his older brother in the 1970s, Gordie found motivation from his younger sibling.

"There's no question that Danny was his inspiration," Gordy said. "But I wondered if Gordie starting at sixteen would be fighting an uphill battle. We had already lost two years of potential when Gordie jumped into this."

Although Gordie began late, hard work compensated for lost time. Soon it became a family tradition that training began when a boy reached eighth grade. In a short time, Chris, Rob, and Goose were looking forward to that benchmark.

Gordy supervised the fitness program, making sure his kids performed safely.

"The key was light weights and a lot of reps," he said. "I never maxed out my boys. Once they got comfortable and had the right form, I moved them up, increasing by two and a half or five pounds at a time. When they performed an exercise the correct way without struggling, I moved them up again. I never had them do anything that could hurt them or cause injury."

When it came to increasing their speed, Gordy sent them to a specialist. He had heard about a former NFL player in the area who trained high schoolers.

Demeris Johnson played for the Miami Dolphins from 1992 to 1996, then spent training camp with the Buffalo Bills before his career ended. Wondering what to do after football, Johnson began using his experience to help younger relatives work out and increase their speed and strength to improve on-field performance. When word of mouth spread, he opened a business.

"Basically, I brought the training methodology that I received at the pro level down to the high school level," Johnson said. "The tag line for my business was, 'To perform like a pro, you must train like a pro.' I brought the intensity that a professional athlete should bring to his work."

At the time, a group of boys trained at West Seneca West High School, where Johnson's son attended school. He quickly gained a reputation for overseeing intense workouts. Speed, agility, strength, and power development were vital. Gordie recalled that many boys found themselves stooped over, winded, even throwing up.

"My goal was to get guys to quit," Johnson noted. "If you got through my training, you could last through any type of adversity that you might face on a field. It wasn't only about the exercises. I tried to help young athletes accomplish their dreams, because I was one of them once and know what it's like to succeed at a high level."

Like any concerned father, Gordy was initially skeptical of Johnson, wanting to meet him to see firsthand what the program was like before he committed. The two spoke via phone, and Johnson suggested Gronkowski bring the boys for a one-day trial. With his four oldest in tow, Gordy oversaw a morning workout in a small, steamy wrestling room at West Seneca West High School.

"I wanted to see if he was just a moneymaking guy, someone who grabs quick cash and goes," Gordy said. "I didn't want my kids training the wrong way. I wanted to make sure he knew it. With my background, I knew a lot of it, but didn't always have the time to do it. Once I saw how he trained, he was exactly what I was looking for."

One session was enough to convince Gordy that Johnson knew his stuff.

"That was our introduction to each other," Johnson recalled. "Afterward, he shook my hand and said, 'You're the man.' It was later on when we sat down and talked about goals for his boys. Gordy became a good friend of mine. I gleaned tips from him and came to respect his business savvy."

Gordie recalled that summer of 2002. He had completed his freshman year on the baseball team at Jacksonville University and knew that he needed to take the next step in his development.

"I had grown three inches that year and needed to improve my footwork to become quicker, more athletic, and get a better step off the bag at first base," he said. "My brothers were doing a training course for football, so I joined in. We worked three or four days a week. By the end of summer, I'd never been in better shape. I lost fifteen pounds of pure fat. My body was ripped and cut. My flexibility was better."

Johnson's program helped develop fast-twitch muscles. He taught the boys correct running form, with hips aligned and arms pumping. He showed the importance of proper footwork and keeping muscles loose.

"A warm-up alone was like a whole day of running," Gordie said. "That's how intense this was. One day we did four-hundred-yard sprints around the track. Other times, it was shorter, one-hundred-meter sprints. Another test was a contest to see how fast you could get off a starting line, twenty times. We also did ladder drills, then worked abs afterward. It was one of the most ridiculous workouts I'd ever seen."

For Gordie, results were immediate. He had greater endurance and appeared more fit. When he returned to Jacksonville, coaches were impressed with the improvement. The year before, he had been slower than his teammates. Now he was among the fastest. With a grin, Gordie mentioned an added bonus: girls noticed his bigger muscles and sculpted abs, approaching him on the beaches in Florida that fall.

"The cool thing is that I was motivated by my brothers, you know?" Gordie said. "We did it together. I was nineteen, Danny was seventeen, Chris was fifteen, and Rob was thirteen. Glenn was too young, but he did the program later. It was hard work but worth it, because we're all such big guys that we needed to learn our bodies. With the sun beating down and sweat pouring off us, the first thing we did when we left the track was stop at a gas station and pound Gatorades."

In typical bragging-rights fashion, Gordie is quick to point out that by summer's end, he was the fastest of his brothers. Johnson confirms this, adding that Gordie was also older and had a year of college training.

"Gordie was faster and would tease all his brothers that he was better," Johnson said. "The Gronkowskis were very competitive. They used to go at it pretty good."

Despite his initial skepticism, Gordy never had second thoughts about Johnson's training. He remains impressed with the gains his boys made.

"Demeris worked with their feet every day, jumping rope and doing crossovers and plyometric boxes," Gordy said. "It was done the right way, not so kids would be lying on the ground, thinking, 'No pain, no gain.' It was a different way of training. At the end, after they all trained with Demeris, Gordie was the fastest. He had been running a five-six [forty-yard dash], but all of a sudden he dropped a second off that. He ran a four-six after smacking a baseball. I couldn't believe it. That kind of gain is amazing and makes a huge difference to an athlete."

The current family home has an expansive basement, with a pool table and five giant wooden trophy cases, featuring memorabilia from each boy's career. Behind sliding glass doors are footballs propped on tees, scores painted near the laces. Various team helmets, jerseys, and game programs are arrayed on shelves. It is the type of display that might be found inside a hall of fame. Gordy updates the contents regularly, and the boys love looking at evidence of their achievements.

Across the concrete floor, on the far size of the room, sit more than two-dozen angled benches and workout machines. Stray free weights and metal clips litter the floor, towels draped from the edges of bars. There are swaths of rubber mats, and the G&G Fitness logo is painted on a wooden base supporting a squat rack. Under a glass-block window, near white-backed insulation, hooks protrude from the walls. On them are stretched leather back supports and dangling jump ropes.

This is where the boys pushed themselves and each other.

"When the boys were growing up, we were in the basement every day," Gordy said. "When Danny and Gordie started lifting together, the other guys got excited and started working out with each other."

With the boys pushing one another, Gordy stepped back to let them develop. All were motivated by competition, not by their father preaching to them. Gradually, Gordy found himself less of a factor in their daily workouts. That was fine with him, because it freed up his time.

Sometimes friends were invited into the workout circle, but none proved to be as committed as the five Gronkowski brothers.

Often a friend would want to work out with one of the boys, so they would set up a regular schedule, but the friend would last only a few weeks before giving up. "Some people just aren't into it," Gordy said. "It takes time and energy. I told the kids if they wanted to take it to the next level, they needed to keep ahead of everybody else. How do you do that? You work out in the basement."

Regardless of workouts, many experts agree that the most important factor in health and fitness is nutrition. Putting the proper fuel into a body has more of an effect than heavy weight training. It's why all the Gronkowskis watch what they eat.

"You get energy from eating the right food and exercising," Gordy said. "What you put into your body is important. Our family developed a diet around protein and glutamine. Potato chips and dip and all that stuff went out of my diet. Very seldom do you catch me eating chicken wings. I stay away from anything greasy."

Even today, in his early fifties, Gordy is a stickler for nutrition.

"I have a protein shake every morning for breakfast, and I exercise for at least twenty minutes. Weights help with definition and keeping things strong, but now I'm not lifting to get big. I don't lift heavy at all. I just try to maintain. I use light weights and good form to keep everything from falling apart. Plus I add in cardio two times per week."

Training and nutrition were integral parts of the Gronkowskis' success. But they weren't the only factors. Sibling rivalry played a part, as did their father's mindset. He used to clip inspiring quotes from athletes, coaches, and other successful people, attaching them to the refrigerator door. The boys read them over each time they went for a snack.

There were words of wisdom from coaching great Vince Lombardi, suggesting that second place is for losers. Another: "Perseverance: it's not whether you get knocked down, it's whether you get back up."

Gordy also employed "teachable moments." When the kids watched sporting events on TV and were inspired by a crushing block, a fluid run, or a diving pass reception, Gordy reminded them that success was a product of hard work. When the boys cheered, Gordy knew he had a captive audience.

"You think that guy got there by watching TV?" Gordy chided. "No, he got there by training. You guys are good, but what's going to take you to the next level is getting into that basement."

Years later, Gordy smiles at the memories, amazed at how far his sons have come. All the workouts were done with an eye to the future.

"My goal in life was to get them to college and get that paid for," he said. "It's the whole reason we started training. Anything after that was a bonus."

Gordie playing summer baseball in the Cape Cod League.

Young Gordie Gronkowski.

4

Gordie Jr.: Doesn't He Know the Rest of the Family Plays Football?

"I'm the only brother in the world who can say he has three younger brothers playing in the NFL."

— GORDIE GRONKOWSKI, JR.

I N THE FALL OF 2011, Gordie Gronkowski, Jr., returned to Western New York for a few days before preparing to make yet another move—this time it was Ohio—where a new phase of his life was set to begin. He had recently finished the baseball season with the Southern Illinois Miners of the Frontier League. The team made the playoffs and he'd batted .308 on the season.

Coming home was a time to catch up with old friends, play golf, see his family, and eat Mom's food. The highlight of his weekend was watching younger brother Rob catch seven passes for one hundred yards, including two touchdowns, when New England visited Ralph Wilson Stadium to play the Bills.

Standing at six feet six inches, wearing a backwards baseball cap lettered with "Gronk Nation," Gordie nodded to his youngest brother, Glenn, ten years his junior, pecking at a computer in the family room.

"What's up, Bro?" Gordie asked. "Is there any food?"

It is a question asked often among the Gronkowski boys. Weighing 250 pounds, with wide shoulders and a posture that belies his history of back injuries, Gordie wore plaid shorts and a white T-shirt that revealed big biceps. On each wrist was a silicone band advertising the family website. He hunted through the refrigerator, discovering a foil tray filled with breaded chicken and rice, a personal favorite — Mom's homemade chicken soufflé. Within seconds, he was spooning it into his mouth.

At twenty-eight, Gordie was more than ten years removed from high school graduation. The past decade had been a whirlwind of success and setbacks, of achievement and injuries. In 2001, he walked onto the baseball team at Jacksonville University, honed his skills, and became a power hitter and star first baseman. After redshirting, he had an outstanding first year, in which he was a freshman All-American and named Freshman of the Year in the conference, before a back injury derailed his steep ascent. But he rehabilitated the ruptured disk, fighting his way back to success. After his senior year, Gordie was drafted by the Los Angeles Angels, only to suffer a recurrence of pain. Since then, the injury had alternately flared then minimized.

Throughout his career, Gordie remained mentally tough and continued to work, playing baseball in ten cities, several more than once.

By the fall of 2011, with the summer season a memory, he planned a move to Cincinnati, yet another city, his eleventh new home in the past ten years. His business degree was about to be put to use: he planned to run several of the family's businesses in Ohio, where G&G Fitness is known as The Fitness Store.

This was a major demarcation in his life. Barring any unforeseen shift, he will not play professional baseball again. But he left the game on his terms.

Many athletes find it hard to walk away from the sport they love. Like addicts, they keep being drawn back. For examples, look no further than Brett Favre or Dominik Hasek, men who attempted comebacks despite being past their prime, with an eye on one final shot at glory. That fall, Gordie was mostly content with his decision to leave the game that has defined his life.

"I'm twenty-eight," he mused. "I've pretty much accomplished everything I can. If I hurt my back again, I'd be pretty upset."

So that's it? Baseball is really done?

Hesitation crept into his voice, but only for a moment, replaced by resolve.

"You know, I probably . . . I probably . . . I'm happy where I am right now. I did everything I wanted to do. This is the perfect year to go out, after six years of being a professional. I had a great year with Southern Illinois. We made the playoffs, even though we ended up losing. I'm happy and the back is healthy. The third game this year, I fouled a pitch off my foot and was in a walking boot for three weeks. I thought, you've got to be kidding. A year ago, I wondered if I should have come back for another year, so I was second-guessing myself. Right now I'm looking forward to joining the real world. I like a new challenge, and working for Pops is a great opportunity."

Paychecks in the independent league are puny, which was another reason for his decision. Still, his words betrayed a hint of wavering.

"I'm probably done, even if someone calls with a good offer. Seeing my brothers succeed will take my mind right back into sports."

While a teenager, Gordie was a star athlete in high school, yet remained unsure of his future. As graduation approached in 2001, his parents encouraged him to start making decisions about life.

"Mom and Dad asked what I wanted to do," he said. "I'm the oldest son, but I was a shy kid. I didn't know about a job or career."

Both his parents dispute Gordie's claim to shyness.

"Gordie loves people," said his mother, Diane. "I used to joke when he played baseball that I was going to keep track of how many hitters got on base, because that's how many guys were coming to dinner that night. Gordie stood there and talked to everyone who made it onto first base. He learned their life story. Everybody was his friend."

It was through those games that Gordie formulated a career plan.

"I liked baseball and thought I could keep playing," he said.

Harking back to his own days as a high school athlete seeking admission to a college program, Gordy knew his son needed to get serious. Bill Hurley, a former teammate of Gordy's at Syracuse and part owner of a company called Collegiate Scouting Network, helped the Gronkowskis create a profile for Gordie to query colleges. The one-page sheet included a headshot and vital statistics like height and weight, academic information, and details about Gordie's successes at baseball.

Father and son located a periodical from 1999 listing more than fourteen hundred men's collegiate baseball programs throughout the United States that offered scholarships. Today most of this information could be tracked online, but they were working at the dawn of the Internet age. They began a systematic approach and contacted colleges that caught their interest.

"Each night we read through a few entries," Gordy recalled. "We found the coach's name and then crafted a letter and faxed it to him. The next day, when Gordie got home from school, he made a follow-up phone call. I showed him how to do the first one, then left him alone to sink or swim."

At first Gordie was nervous about phoning a coach, unsure if he was saying the right things. But the experience forced him to become more outgoing and self-reliant. A decade later, he believes the process made him a better person.

"I didn't know how to do any of that stuff," Gordie said. "A follow-up call? What does that even mean? But my dad taught me that other people can only do so much for you. If you want to achieve, you have to do it yourself, because you don't always know what others are doing. Are coaches really calling scouts on your behalf? I started to feel more comfortable with each call."

In the course of four weekends, father and son traveled to eighteen colleges, setting off on a Thursday and returning the following Sunday. They visited various areas of the country and tried to squeeze in as many meetings as possible.

"We got in the car with a stack of videos we had made,"

Gordie said. "We were looking for colleges that would give me an opportunity to play."

New Haven, Central Connecticut, and Ithaca were one weekend. Ohio State, Liberty College, Richmond, and Virginia Commonwealth were another. Eventually, they ended up in the South. As they ventured farther from home, Gordie became more disillusioned.

"We weren't getting much feedback," he admitted. "We were in Florida and planned to spend a day at the beach, but it was pouring rain. We figured, we're here to visit colleges, so let's go to Jacksonville. I had contacted them and received a return letter."

An assistant coach at Jacksonville University was a fellow northerner, from Michigan, also a large man. Joe Fletcher took one look at Gordie. Perhaps seeing a younger reflection of himself, he was intrigued.

"OK, so you're a big boy," Fletcher said. "Can you swing a bat?"

"Yeah," Gordie smiled. "I can do all right."

NCAA rules prohibit tryouts for a college team. But no such rules apply to community colleges. Gordie found himself at nearby Tallahassee Community College, a powerhouse at its level. After smacking the ball in impressive fashion, Gordie was offered a spot with Tallahassee.

"That's when I knew I had something to work with," he said. "Jacksonville was one of the few programs to show any interest. They gave me the opportunity, and I took advantage of that."

Gordie arrived at Jacksonville University in September 2001 as a walk-on first baseman. His redshirt year proved a valuable time to become acclimated to college baseball. Redshirting is common in collegiate sports, particularly football.

"When you go into your freshman year, there's a good possibility that you're not going to play, or you need more time to develop," he explained. "As a redshirt, you train and practice and do everything with the team, but you don't play in games unless another kid gets hurt. That way, your second year becomes your freshman year."

In the interim, Gordie grew three inches, to six feet six, and added nearly thirty pounds. He also became accustomed to a year-round schedule. Teammates from the South played baseball for twelve months, and their output showed. Contrast that to Gordie's senior year of high school, when he competed in only fifteen games. Back in Jacksonville in fall 2002, he was ready to perform on the field. But nothing was handed to him.

"I sat the first nineteen games," Gordie recalled. "There was another freshman ahead of me who was a lefty. There's a little advantage for a guy who bats left and plays first base because it's easier for him to catch the ball. He had an advantage, but it came down to skills, attitude, and mental toughness."

When his fellow first baseman struggled with hitting, Gordie was inserted into the lineup. Butterflies and nerves got the best of him for a few innings until he calmed himself and focused on fundamentals.

"My shortstop threw me a two-seamer and the ball took off, moving across the diamond at more than ninety miles per hour," Gordie recalled of his first college game. "It hit me in the chest and I was credited with an error. Then I struck out in my first at-bat. The next one, I hit a laser to left field, but it was caught, so now I'm oh-for-two with an error. My first game, and I'm embarrassed already. It was terrible. I believed this was my opportunity to shine."

In his third at-bat, Gordie recorded a single, and later added a double, to finish the day 2-4. He felt redeemed, and in typical Gronkowski fashion, focused on the positives.

"Bat five hundred and you make it to the Hall of Fame," he preached.

But Gordie found himself returned to the bench for another two games before an opportunity to pinch-hit in the seventh inning against rival North Florida.

"We were down five to two at the time, two outs and a guy on second," Gordie said. "I got a hit and my first RBI. It was a huge situation and I responded. Now I'm three-for-five. In the next game, I was given a chance to play and went three-for-four. That was it. I played the rest of my career."

"His first year, he was just learning," confirmed Terry Alexander, Jacksonville University's baseball coach. "First base is a really difficult position to play and be good at. At this level, guys are throwing in the high eighties across the diamond and into the dirt. Balls are coming off aluminum bats at one hundred miles per hour, and you've got to field it. You can stick a tall guy over there to catch it in the air, but you better have a good athlete, because it's a very demanding position. That position can win or lose a lot of games. If the ball bounces off your glove, maybe the shortstop gets the error, but you've lost the game. A good first baseman eliminates that error."

By season's end, Gordie had been named Freshman All-American, Freshman of the Year in the Atlantic Sun Conference, and most valuable player of the conference tournament. The team advanced to regionals before losing to Florida State.

"I was the youngest guy on the team, and I was a part of our success. I was batting fourth where power hitters swing. Everything came together and I was thinking, Wow. Maybe I won't graduate college. Maybe I'll get drafted before then!"

Because of his strong season, Gordie was invited to play in Topeka, Kansas, in the Jayhawk League of summer collegiate teams. He was excited about the prospect of playing summer baseball and living with a host family. But after only three games, a twinge in his right leg grew into cause for concern.

"Something wasn't feeling right," Gordie said. "I had been playing baseball year round and thought I was just burned out. It was a tweak and I was frustrated, but figured I better let my coach know about it."

After consulting with his coach, Gordie reached a decision: he would take the summer off from the sport to rest his body and prepare for his sophomore year in September. So in 2003, he returned to Western New York. But the rest didn't last long. He trained with his brothers under the tutelage of Demeris Johnson.

Although no one knew it, somewhere along the way Gordie had ruptured a disk between his lumbar and sacrum. This is a painful injury, but paradoxically, when he worked out, the hurt diminished. So he kept exercising.

"You feel better after a workout because things get stretched and the nerve isn't pressing against the liquid that squirted from the disk," Gordie explained. "I started doing heavier squats, heavier bench presses, and I felt good."

During the fall of his third year in Jacksonville—his sophomore season—he continued to train with the team, competing in intrasquad practices. During second semester, as baseball season approached, the pain flared again.

"I felt good during workouts, but once I got home, everything tightened up," he said. "I had trouble sitting in class. I wasn't sleeping. When I'd go out to have a few drinks with my buddies, I felt worse, because alcohol dried my body out. But I kept playing and started the season. I was twenty years old and coming off a ridiculous freshman year. I didn't want to let anyone know what was going on if I could tolerate the pain."

Nerves tingled down his right leg, stretching from knee to heel. On the field, he struggled to hit the ball. After twenty games, it was time to see a trainer.

"I probably should have gone earlier, but I just don't know," Gordie lamented, shaking his head. "Anyone who has had back pain can appreciate how weird it is. I didn't think it was my back. I thought it was my leg, because the pain was going down my right side. But trainers thought I had a herniated disk, so I was sent for an MRI. The results came back that I completely blew it out."

Gordie was given the option to play through the pain. Doctors assured him that no further damage would result by continuing to play baseball. But the coaches recognized Gordie's daily struggles.

"I talked to Mom and Dad," he said. "How much pain am I supposed to take? I couldn't sit through a class. I wasn't enjoying my regular, everyday life, let alone baseball. After examining all the options, my parents suggested that I should get this taken care of."

Within a week, the surgeon for the Jacksonville Jaguars operated on Gordie, cutting a tiny slit into his back. Jelly from the ruptured disk, which had been pushing against nerves, was dissolved using high-intensity lasers.

"It was a simple surgery and I was in and out," Gordie said. "Mom came down for Easter 2004. She helped me that first week, because I couldn't really walk. I couldn't carry books or anything for a while. I had to let that disk heal again, and you hope that it does."

Years later, Gordie looks back with second thoughts. He realizes now that perhaps he rushed back to baseball too quickly. Jacksonville was not in contention to compete in regionals his sophomore year, but he played the final fifteen games that season, returning less than two months after surgery.

"It's great to have goals and dreams," he said. "But sometimes it's better to take a step back and get your body healthy again. At the time, all I wanted to do was play sports. I was a young kid thinking I had a shot at the major league."

His father reflects on that time with frustration, wondering how things might have aligned differently if Gordie had rested more.

"Gordie had a knucklehead strength coach at Jacksonville," Gordy said. "Once you have back surgery, you have to lay off. You need to stay still for six weeks. You can walk, but never bend. You can't turn. You get out of bed a certain way. Gordie did all that, but this idiot put him on weights right away. You don't strengthen a disk. It's not a muscle. You got to let the damn thing heal totally and then work on core strength. Stretch the hamstrings. This guy had him doing stupid things that didn't help. When he played, it flared up, because at first base you're always bending."

"I wasn't one hundred percent ready," Gordie admitted. "Mentally, I wanted to play, but physically, it just wasn't there. My plan that summer was to come back to Buffalo to rehab and get my back right. I had no plans for summer ball unless I got a call from Cape Cod."

Like many young baseball players, Gordie considered the Cape Cod Baseball League his best opportunity to spend a summer. Pitchers hurled balls at speeds approaching one hundred miles per hour. Scouts attended nearly every game. The collegiate league's atmosphere was exciting. There was no box office or ticket window. Fans simply laid a towel on a hillside surrounding the field to claim their spot, and a bucket was passed asking for loyalty contributions, suggested at three dollars per person. People sometimes jockeyed for a choice swatch of lawn the day before a heated contest.

"I got a voicemail from a coach who asked if I would play first base," Gordie said. "Coming off surgery, I hadn't finished my sophomore season too strong, so I did not expect that call. But when it came, I knew right away that I had to take advantage of the opportunity."

Although Gordie was released from the league after three weeks, he speaks fondly of the experience. It was his first time living with a host family. He admired many of the guys alongside whom he played. And always, along the way, he kept learning his sport. There were different situations, different signs for stealing bases, techniques to hitting the ball and getting a jump on a base run. Gordie tried to take a little piece from each experience and adapt it to his game.

"It was cool to see how that league worked. I was let go because I was struggling, but just to say I was part of it was an accomplishment. It left me knowing what I needed to do to get better."

During the summer of 2004, Gordie wasn't idle long. Another call came requesting his services — this one from the Torrington Twisters of the New England Collegiate Baseball League.

"There were really good players there, too," Gordie said. "Our shortstop, Eli Iorg, was drafted in the first round. I had a good year there, batting over three hundred. That got my confidence back up. I went into my junior year of college thinking I had a shot at getting drafted."

Away from the baseball diamond, success in academics began to take root. He had started his college career at Jacksonville as a walk-on, receiving no scholarship. Because his father was a successful businessman, there was no financial aid either. Attending college cost $23,000 per year.

"My dad cut a deal with me," Gordie said. "If I got a three-point-oh, he would pay for half my schooling. But I battled in the classroom just to be a B student. I don't have the intelligence that my brothers Chris or Danny have. They're very book smart, but I'm better talking to people."

During his first and second years at college, Gordie did not reach the 3.0 benchmark, and he lamented his growing debt. But in his junior year, he finally earned that grade, and his father made good on the promise. Also, because of his strong play on the baseball diamond, Gordie received a partial academic scholarship. Financially, attending college became less stressful. Now it was time to prove it on the baseball diamond.

"I had a solid junior season," he said. "I hit three thirty-three, which is pretty good, and had an on-base percentage of over four hundred. I was hoping to hear my name get called in the draft, but nothing happened. I wondered what I needed to do to get drafted. I think my back surgery scared a lot of teams away."

In the summer of 2005, Gordie returned to the Torrington Twisters for summer ball, where he batted over .300 again. During his senior year at Jacksonville, the numbers became even more impressive: a batting average of .370, ten home runs, and seventy RBIs.

"He had a great senior year," said Alexander, the coach at Jacksonville. "To put it in perspective, I had two players on that team who were first-team all-conference players, one of whom, Daniel Murphy, was player of the year and is in the big leagues now with the Mets. Yet Gordie was the MVP on our team. Without a doubt, he was the leader of the club. He was good in the locker room and carried himself well. He had a lot to do with our winning the championship that year."

There was a lighthearted side to Gordie as well. His coach recalled that Gordie often did not understand his own strength.

"He'd hit a home run and give someone a high-five and just about knock the guy's shoulder out of its socket," Alexander said. "People started elbow-bumping him because otherwise they wouldn't be able to play the next day. Gordie didn't mean to, but he was like a big Labrador retriever who got so excited."

After another championship ring, Gordie believed he would be drafted.

"After the season, I talked to scouts, filled out forms, received a stack of letters," he said. "All indications were I'd be drafted in the middle rounds, somewhere between twenty and thirty. It's strange, but my mindset changed after the surgery. I just wanted to finish college and have a chance to play."

In 2006, Gordie earned a business degree from Jacksonville. That June, he watched the baseball draft on TV at his friend's house, growing more frustrated as each team passed him by. Thirty-two teams each draft fifty rounds, hoping to stock their rosters with talent. With each passing team, Gordie heard a different name than his. Round thirty-five came and went. Then forty. Then forty-five.

"That's when I left the room," Gordie said. "My buddy told me that I just got drafted in the forty-ninth round. My dad was the first one to phone. Five minutes later I got a call from the Los Angeles Angels' recruiting director."

Baseball insiders confirm that Gordie's back problems were a red flag to professional teams.

"Most teams are going to shy away from a back problem," Alexander said. "Back problems are the main reason why Gordie isn't playing in games that are on TV."

As part of his path to the major league, Gordie traveled to Orem, Utah, and played eight games for the Orem Owlz.

"We drafted Gordie and he did very well for us," said Tom Kotchman, a longtime scout for the Los Angeles Angels who works out of Florida. His son, Casey, is a star first baseman who played the 2011 season with the Tampa Bay Rays. "Gordie is a big target at first base. He's imposing, and he hits with power."

Kotchman also coaches young men who sign into the organization, so he was familiar with Gordie both on and off the field.

"Gordie was a fifth-year senior, which means he was twenty-two or twenty-three when he came to us, so he was a year or two older than some of the other kids. Because of his size and ability, he was a perfect guy to have on the club. He was a leader by example. He was a great role model for other kids to follow on how to act like a professional. Probably the hardest thing for him was taking bus rides, because when you're that size, you don't easily fit in those rows. At six six, that was tough."

Batting at .287 in Orem, Gordie was just finding a rhythm when his back went out.

"We were playing in Casper, Wyoming, and the owner flew me back in his private plane," Gordie said. "I was done for the season. I figured they were going to let me go, but I did rehab for three or four hours each day, working my abs, spending time in the pool. I worked my ass off, hoping to get another opportunity."

It came the following season, when he returned to Orem. During spring training, he was on an extended plan where he did not draw a paycheck but remained on the bench, hoping to be moved into the lineup. Shortly, he had earned his way back to a roster spot, and his game returned to the level he anticipated.

"This was the best time of my life," Gordie recalled. "I hit three forty-four that season, was top five in every category, and my back was one hundred percent. I played first base and batted fourth. We won it all that year, and it was my first minor-league ring. I had a big role on that team and it was unbelievable to be part of something again. Having worked through that adversity, it was a great feeling."

The following season Gordie started playing Single A baseball in Cedar Rapids, Iowa, the affiliate for the Los Angeles Angels. With a cold and rainy start to the season, his back grew tight, flaring again. He hit .220, the worst of his career, and after three months of rehab, was released.

"That's how it all ended, but I thanked everyone I ever worked with," he said. "They did not have to give me a chance to rehab, to pay me to get healthy and live my life. I ended up playing another three years of professional independent ball, but I never had another chance to be picked up by the major league."

In 2009, Gordie played in Avon, Ohio, outside Cleveland, for the Lake Erie Crushers of the Frontier League. He was named team captain.

"I had never played close to home before, so that was great," he reflected. "There were twelve teams in the league, and all the others were established. We were a first-year club that won it all. I got another fat ring for that."

The following summer, he was traded to Worcester, Massachusetts, located near Foxborough. Worcester was interested in Gordie for an obvious marketing connection: little brother Rob had just been drafted by the New England Patriots, and by all accounts Rob was going to be a star.

"They thought the name recognition was a reason to bring me in," Gordie explained. "But it was a very different experience. Their field was at Holy Cross. All the players lived in a huge dorm room that was like a frat hole. The guys on that team were with each other day and night. I was used to staying with a host family and having time to myself. Also, I wasn't playing that much."

The team's coach, Rich Gedman, had been a catcher for the Boston Red Sox. He admitted to Gordie that other teams had inquired about adding him to their roster.

"Gedman was straight-up honest with me, which I liked," Gordie said. "He thought I should be playing somewhere instead of sitting on the bench. So I was traded to Gateway, outside St. Louis, for the second half of the season."

From there the moves came fast and furious. Gateway traded Gordie back to Worcester, which then shipped him out for a second stint in Lake Erie. The Crushers waited until the off-season to send him to Southern Illinois, where he played the 2011 season.

By September 2011, Gordie believed his career had come to a close.

"Truth is, I enjoyed independent ball. It's only ninety games, whereas in the minor leagues you're playing a hundred and fifty or sixty. Ninety games in a hundred days was perfect for my back."

Despite Gordie's claims that he is done with professional baseball at twenty-eight, his father wonders if the final chapter has been written on his son's athletic achievements.

"Gordie has a great story," his father claimed proudly. "It's a shame he had to have back surgery. He did everything he had to do to be successful. He never quit, just kept going and going."

"An injury like that can't help your career," said Kotchman, the Angels' scout and coach at Orem. "For sports like baseball or golf, you're supplying a lot of torque there. That's tough, especially when you're Gordie's size."

Glenn Gronkowski, speaking about his nephew and brother, reflected on the big picture.

"I always pictured Gordie a little like his father," he said. "Gordie was kind of the goof-off type. Then I went to one of his college baseball games and he had gotten so much better. I don't know why he never got a legit tryout after he was drafted. I don't understand the politics behind baseball. When I saw him playing outside Cleveland, he was batting over three hundred. That kid had a wicked stick. He sure could put the ball over the fence."

Kotchman has overseen the development of many young men over the years, but Gordie remains memorable for more than his achievements in baseball.

"Gordie is someone you'll never forget," Kotchman said. "Guys with his makeup stand out. You never had to worry about Gordie on or off the field. He always dressed well and spoke well and presented himself professionally. I didn't have anything to do with that. That's just the way he was. Gordie will be successful in whatever he decides to do. He'll be a leader in life."

Although his sport of choice was different from that of his four brothers, Gordie believes that he set a standard for the younger boys to follow.

"Even though I didn't go the football route, I think my experiences made it easier for my brothers to leave home when the time came," he mused. "Now that it looks like baseball is done, people ask how I feel. I feel great. I'm the only brother in the world who can say he has three younger brothers playing in the NFL. My littlest brother is going to Kansas State on a full scholarship and maybe heading to the NFL, so someday soon there may be four. I'm their biggest fan."

Competition, however, still runs deep in the family roots. As he finished eating the chicken soufflé he laid down his fork and leaned forward.

"Just make sure to mention that I have more rings than all my brothers combined," Gordie said with a grin. "I have four. Two from college, one from my first year in pro ball, and another from my first year in independent ball. So I must have done something right along the way."

Rob's bandage — "Hard Work" — says it all.

Dan, Rob, Chris, and their father check out the Wall of Fame in their high school's weight room, 2012.
Photo by Jeff Schober

5

Mental Toughness

"More than anything, mentality and the approach to preparation are the keys to making it."

— DEMERIS JOHNSON,
TRAINER AND FORMER NFL PLAYER

TALK TO ANY OF THE Gronkowskis, and the phrase "mental toughness" is routinely repeated. Gordie described the behind-the-scenes preparation required to be a great baseball player. Dan echoed those sentiments regarding football and mentioned there was some indefinable factor that the brothers each possess.

"We were blessed with our size," Dan mused, "and obviously something went on in the house where we're all mentally tough."

Their father trained his boys to follow the golden rule but to do so with a stubborn streak.

"I instilled in all my kids that you never quit," Gordy said. "If you start something in life, you have to finish it. When they were young, my boys were on teams where they would come home and complain that they didn't like it. Well, guess what? You finish it. They would say that they didn't like the coach. I told them, so what? You finish it. You're going to meet people in life you don't like, but part of being successful is that you work around it."

Being a former NFL player himself, Demeris Johnson immediately recognized traits in the Gronkowski brothers that could lead to athletic accomplishment. They possessed physical gifts but also had the proper mindset for success.

As a trainer, Johnson has developed a keen eye for temperament and talent. During their initial workouts together in the summer of 2002, Johnson knew he was dealing with special players.

"I can't say whether an athlete will make it to the big time or not, because there are so many determining factors in that," he reflected. "But what I do recognize — and I can pick it up like that — is whether a kid has what it takes to make it. I can tell if a boy has the potential to make it. When I saw Robbie, I recognized he had the potential to be the best tight end in the nation."

What makes the difference between an average athlete and an elite athlete?

"More than anything, mentality and the approach to preparation are the keys to making it," Johnson said. "A lot of kids don't understand that. Their father had already done a wonderful job in giving them the mentality they needed to prepare for greatness. Once I saw that, it was easy. I just had to apply the methodology."

Gordy reflected on the way he raised his sons.

"I preached motivational skills all the time. If you're motivated and keep driving at something, then everything good will happen."

The refrigerator remains the central appliance in the Gronkowski home. When all the boys lived under one roof, the weekly food bill exceeded $600. The refrigerator door was opened and closed more times than anyone can count. Gordy knew this was one spot where his sons focused their attention. So he taped inspirational quotes there, knowing every time a growing palm was laid against its handle, his boys would be unwittingly exposed to a burst of wisdom.

One of Gordy's favorites, saved over the years: "Teamwork is the most important concept in sports. Together everyone achieves more. The true team has trust, love, commitment, and belief in one another."

And, from UCLA basketball coach John Wooden: "Ability may get you to the top. But it takes character to keep you there."

"That whole refrigerator was coated with quotes," Gordy said. "Every little space was filled. If I stumbled across something good when I was reading, I put the quote up there. I also added articles where people did something stupid . . . pro athletes whose career ended over stupidity. The message was: Don't be this guy. Don't do this. You're no better than anybody else. Don't start thinking you are. You've just been gifted with different traits than others. I preached and preached that."

Gordy knew he went overboard when the boys complained they were tired of another new quote on the refrigerator door.

"I reached a point where I was probably overdoing it," Gordy said with a laugh. "But something must have worked, because all the boys have become successful in their own right. Even now, Goose still has a couple of them taped to the wall in his bedroom."

Toughness is a common strand in their family lore.

"I don't know if I should tell this story," Gordy admitted. "But one time when they were kids, Danny came home from school upset because there was a bully picking on him on the bus."

Diane, the boys' mother, listened with concern, then instructed her son to alert the bus driver if the bullying happened again. Gordy grew quiet, waiting until his wife had left the room to call his boys over. He asked Gordie if he had been there when his younger brother was picked on. Gordie admitted timidly that he had.

"You're family," Gordy told the two boys, using thick fingers to punctuate his words. "You need to jump in and protect one another. If this kid does it again tomorrow, you both jump in and beat the living shit out of him."

Years later, Gordy remembers the difficult instructions he gave his sons.

"Maybe that wasn't the right way to do it. But in my opinion that was the right thing to do at the time. I don't take crap from anybody, and I didn't want my boys to either. I taught them not to start trouble but not to take it either. Treat people the way you want to be treated. I bring up the word 'karma' all the time. If you screw people or steal from others, it's going to come back to bite you three times harder. My boys learned to do it the right way, and they won't have problems."

• • •

"Professional athletes are really good at kicking themselves in the butt," said Bill Cole, a mental-game coach based in Cupertino, California, near San Jose. "Professional athletes have a sense of sacrifice and can push themselves to do things when they don't want to. There are many guys with the same physical ability who just don't have the drive."

Originally from Western New York, Cole has worked for nearly three decades as a sports-psychology consultant. An acclaimed tennis star himself, Cole is a nationally recognized expert on the mindset of athletes and successful nonathletes. He is the founder and president of the International Mental Game Coaching Association, an organization dedicated to advancing research, development, and growth of mental-game coaching worldwide. He is also the author of numerous books and more than four hundred articles on the subject. He has encountered a wide variety of athletes over a thirty-year professional span.

"A lot of times people reach Division One or the pro level from a war of attrition," he noted. "They don't quit. Other people may have more talent than a pro but didn't want to tolerate the malarkey that goes along with it. They get tired of traveling. They don't like coaches yelling at them. They want to settle down and have a family. There are a host of reasons that a person can lose the motivation to deny himself. You could almost argue that someone has to be fanatical to reach the upper level of sports."

The phrase used by the Gronkowskis, "mental toughness," is one that is familiar to elite athletes. Cole explained that it is a subset of the mental game.

"Mental toughness revolves around several different things," he said. "One is the ability to deny yourself, sacrifice and push yourself in special circumstances, particularly when you're tired or bored or playing through an injury. Suppose conditions are awful; it's windy or hot or cold or whatever. Maybe you're playing against someone who is trying to psych you out or a coach who is abusive. All of these things need to be tolerated, ignored, and pushed past. That's how I would characterize the ability to be mentally tough."

If a person is in a contest against a weak opponent, there may not be much mental toughness required, Cole explained. Yes, focus and self-discipline are needed, but mental toughness becomes evident in the face of difficulties. Family dynamics are an important factor as well.

"Psychologists talk about the concept of 'runs in families,'" Cole said. "Usually it's in the context of mental disorders, but the question is about genetics. Is it passed down from generations as traditions or are they behaviors that get picked up unconsciously? That's probably more the case with mental toughness."

Although he is a Williamsville native, he does not know the Gronkowski family. Yet he was able to generalize about the family based on his experience with successful athletes.

"In this case, you have a father who is a highly successful business owner who needs mental toughness to fulfill his job; plus I would imagine he's a fitness aficionado himself," Cole suggested. "Then you've got all the boys who grew up in that environment. I'm betting the boys had a pretty good dose of that. If their mother reinforced that as well, then the boys were all rough-and-tumble and played sports. Part of their success is probably based on parenting style. When a kid fell down, I'm sure they didn't rush over and hold them and say, 'Johnny, it's going to be okay.' They probably said, 'Suck it up, that's life.' They learned early on to have mental toughness."

Shannon Walton, a mental-skills coach based in Rochester, New York, echoed the importance of family upbringing.

"There are many factors that contribute to an athlete's success," Walton said. "One is the support of the family. Most of the young athletes I work with have extremely supportive parents. The biggest issue is finding the balance between pushing them with high expectations but also being supportive if they have an off game or even an off month."

There are several examples where athletic success is part of the family makeup.

"It's rare, but it's not as rare as everyone thinks," noted Tony Massarotti, a Boston talk show host and writer. "In many ways, it speaks to genetics and upbringing."

Massarotti mentioned examples of three brother-combinations who played Major League Baseball, including J. D., Stephen, and Tim Drew. Also, Vince, Joe, and Dom DiMaggio, and Felipe, Matty, and Jesus Alou. In football, the Manning family is a multigenerational example. Archie was a standout quarterback who raised two Super Bowl winners, Peyton and Eli.

"In every town there is a sports family, and on the grander scale of American sports, there are super sports families," Massarotti said. "Are the Gronkowskis one of them? I don't think there's any question. Talk about proud parenting."

Walton agreed that to achieve at a high level, an athlete must be driven and goal-oriented, with an end target in mind.

"One personality trait that I often find is perfectionism," Walton observed. "It drives and pushes and motivates an athlete, but when they don't hit their mark all the time, which is an unrealistic goal, that can start hurting them. They lose some of their motivation. The most successful athletes are those who find a balance between expecting to work to their ability but understanding they won't be perfect all the time."

What, then, is the biggest difference between a casual athlete or "weekend warrior" and the elites who succeed at high levels of sport?

"For the professional, that is his job, so he has the dedication, perseverance, and will to succeed," Cole noted. "A weekend warrior who played college ball or semipro may look at the long haul and realize it's a lot of work. Suddenly, that office job looks pretty good. He decides to go the other way. The professional is probably the bigger dreamer who can see himself playing pro. The other guy only wishes he could play. Seeing yourself is one thing; wishing it is another. From the neck up, there's the difference."

"I think training mentally gives you an advantage," Gordie said. "You can study it. There are guys who teach you. After I started training mentally, I would actually dream and see the ball coming in. I could see a pitch coming from the pitcher's hand. If it was in the wrong position, I knew I wasn't going to swing."

Gordie's first experience with mental training came during his junior year of college. He and his teammates were instructed to lie down in the outfield while a coach walked among them, urging positive thoughts, encouraging them to visualize the ball as it was pitched. It wasn't until his second year in the minor league, however, that Gordie committed to mental training.

"Baseball is a game of failure," he observed. "If you're playing a great game, you're only going to hit one out of every three pitches, which is crazy. You can be the most talented person but never make it. You have to make yourself ready every single second. When I get up to bat, I clear everything else out of my mind. There is a pitch coming at me at ninety miles per hour. If I lose concentration for a split second, I'm done. The question is, how do you stay mentally focused? That's what makes a great player versus someone who's not.

"Some people don't understand and don't want to believe in mental training. But to me, it's the truth. A lot of guys just want to swing. But ask yourself, where was that pitch? Where did it come out of his hands? If it doesn't come out in the same spot, it could be a ball or a strike. Training mentally gives you an advantage."

Part of the edge, he admitted, is psychological.

"If I train mentally and a pitcher doesn't, I have the advantage every time. That kind of attitude brings positive energy to you and your teammates. If you talk positive to yourself and say that nobody is going to beat you, it will work. I've seen guys in a slump who don't care about the team. They're thinking me, me, and can't figure out why they aren't getting to the next level. It's because they don't have it upstairs. They come in with heads down and they're weak because of it.

"You see guys who throw their bats and helmets. The umpire calls a strike and they act like it's the end of the world. Fans get tired of it. Just get up there and get ready for the next pitch. I always walked up to the plate like I was the best. Whether I had it in me that day or not, I took that approach. Do that every day, and you'll be a good baseball player."

The same foundation applies to any sport. Although he does not underestimate its importance in football, Dan Gronkowski believes that mental toughness is only one element that contributes to being a professional athlete. The most important factor is possessing needed skills.

"I've heard many theories," he said. "You've got to be mentally tough, but you've also got to have it. You can go so far with being mentally tough, but at the end, it comes down to the fact that you have physical skills. Guys can make it through college even if they aren't exceptional players but succeed because they do everything right and get the job done. When it comes to the next step, that's a different story. The NFL is the best of the best. To achieve there, a player must have what it takes. That's where it all comes together."

Being a high school star is one thing, but succeeding in college athletics is more difficult. Achieving at the professional level is a rare accomplishment. Some, like Gordie, despite all his promise, get derailed by injury. Dan and Chris Gronkowski made it to the NFL, where they have played with and against the best of the best. Few attain the level of stardom that Rob achieved in only his second pro season.

But the common components are physical and mental toughness.

• • •

"Football is the roughest game out there," Gordy reflected. "Every Sunday when my boys take the field, I worry and pray that they'll be okay. But getting hurt is part of the game, and they know that."

The family has suffered its share of sports-related injuries. Gordy lost significant time as a college football player thanks to a weight-room injury; Gordie's back likely cost him a shot playing Major League Baseball. Dan strained a hamstring in 2011 that led to him being cut by the New England Patriots, although he was later re-signed. Chris tore a pectoral muscle that ended his 2011 season in Indianapolis. Rob's back injury wiped out most of his junior year of college, while a bad ankle limited him in the Super Bowl. When lining up to block a kick in 2012, he broke his arm and missed several games.

Despite the long list, Gordy looks at his own athletic accomplishments and wouldn't have done anything differently.

"Despite the injuries I had, I would go back and do it all again," he said. "There is a fulfillment in your life when you play sports at a high level. The game lets you live in the limelight for a little bit of time. I remember playing at Ohio State. I looked around the stadium, and there were ninety-four thousand people watching me. It's a remarkable feeling to know that I've been there and done that."

His boys have always thrived on competition. No parent wants to see a child get injured. But playing sports defines who the Gronkowskis are.

"I would take the exact same path as a dad. I can't tell anybody that the game is too crazy or violent. I'd never tell anybody to stop playing. My boys know in their hearts they've done something that not many other people have. They love it. It's in their blood. I have to trust that they'll know when the light goes out and it's time to call it a career."

He points to Gordie, who retired from baseball at twenty-eight. In the ensuing time, his back problems have minimized and he has found comfort in a life after professional sports. The experience, however, is something he will always savor.

"There's just something about the fulfillment of being on a team," Gordy said. "I can sell a ten-thousand-dollar treadmill, and that's a great feeling. But it's nothing like the thrill of putting a guy on his back."

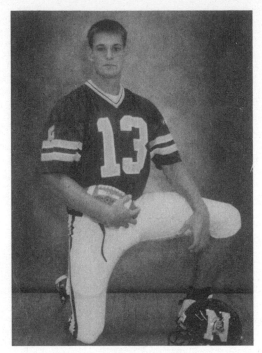

Young Dan Gronkowski. .

Dan played tight end for the Denver Broncos in 2010.

6

Dan: The Talented Workhorse

"There is a whole other side of football that a lot of people don't see."

— DAN GRONKOWSKI

O N A WINDY SPRING AFTERNOON, Dan Gronkowski stood at one end of the oval track, surveying empty terrain. His legs warm and loose from stretching, he inhaled deeply, then began jogging, slowly at first, gaining speed as he rounded the initial turn. Palms clenched into fists, muscled arms pumped, and size-sixteen sneakers pounded against the track as the pace increased.

Dan knew that moments like this were required if he was to succeed at football.

None of his friends accompanied him anymore. Some buddies started training with Dan, but gave up after a few outings. He was too intense, and they did not understand the benefits to extra work. Few shared his commitment, drive, or stamina.

"I need to work harder," Dan thought, completing his first lap.

"I'll put in extra time to really make sure I know what I'm doing."

Soon he was drenched in sweat, maintaining concentration on footwork and the mechanics of running, all details he had been taught over the years. "Keep that cardio up," he thought. "Focus on form."

Make no mistake: Dan is no Forrest Gump, shaking off the proverbial leg braces. He knew he had talent. He had proven that all through high school. Dan was the best athlete on every team he played for.

But he sometimes wondered about the competition that lay beyond Western New York. There were hints as a fourteen-year-old, when he placed second in the nation in the NFL's Punt, Pass, & Kick youth competition. Later, he excelled at the Jim Kelly Football Camp, where the former Buffalo Bills great demonstrated methods to be successful. But the quarterback's teachings came with a warning to student athletes about the long odds of making it to the NFL. Maybe one kid from the camp could end up in the pros, Kelly cautioned. One kid, if he was lucky.

"I'm not going to say it out loud," Dan thought at the time, "but let it be me."

Winded by the third lap, Dan kept pushing. His success was never limited to sports. He brought the same intensity to his studies as well, logging long hours poring over textbooks, forcing himself to master various subjects and impress his teachers. There were smarter kids than him, he knew that, but he vowed that no one would work harder. Any success he had would be achieved the old-fashioned way — he would earn it.

· · ·

"Danny is a fighter," his father reflected. "When he was younger, he dominated, and as he got older, he kept fighting to get to the next level."

The lesson began in eighth grade, when his ankle snapped playing football. That was when his father urged him to begin training in earnest, to get serious about fitness. The injury limited him in certain things, but Dan could lift weights. With an encouraging push from Dad, Dan spent most nights in the basement gym, focusing on proper form and technique to develop his upper body. Soon the results were evident.

At Williamsville North High School, Dan played receiver, starting as a sophomore on the varsity team. The following year, he became the team's quarterback. Gordie, two years older, sometimes practiced catching balls.

"When Danny was the QB, and threw those passes, he just about broke my fingers," Gordie said with a laugh. "I sprained every single one."

According to Mike Mammoliti, Dan's high school coach, Dan was a leader who displayed versatility and football intelligence.

"When I think of Dan Gronkowski, I think about commitment," Mammoliti reflected. "You saw it early on. He wanted to be as good as he could be. He was a consummate team player, almost like a coach on the field. He knew everything that was going on. When he started with us, he played linebacker, then safety, and then quarterback. That's where I really thought he was going to end up."

Mammoliti recalled a funny moment in a high school playoff game against Niagara Falls. The team had just come off the sidelines when Dan trotted toward him.

"What's the play, Coach?" he asked.

Mammoliti told him, then watched the offense gather at center field.

"Dan runs out, calls it in the huddle, gets his hands underneath the center," Mammoliti said. "Suddenly he looks up and calls time-out. He starts smiling as he's walking back toward me."

"What's wrong?" Mammoliti yelled.

Dan's sheepish grin was evident beneath his helmet. "I forgot the play."

Such moments of levity interrupted the intensity Dan brought to the game. During high school, his summers were filled with back-to-back football camps.

"Being our first time through the football cycle, we had no idea what to do," Dan said, referring to his younger brothers' future success. "I went to five football camps every summer just to try to get my name out there. You can only get so much out of each camp, but we didn't know that then. By the time my younger brothers were doing it, my dad had the system down. Chris and Rob and Glenn didn't attend all these football camps for no reason."

While in retrospect his busy summers may have been overkill, the experience did reap dividends.

"It paid off in the end," Dan said. "I went to Maryland's camp three years in a row, and they were one of two schools that offered me anything. That's how I got my scholarship."

In much the same way his father and older brother worked to get themselves recruited, Dan contacted college programs and sent tapes for review. He believes, however, that playing in New

York put him at a disadvantage compared to kids from other regions of the country.

"Coming from this area is tough," he reflected. "Football is kind of behind compared to states like Florida and Texas, where they train year round. Those kids are working all winter and spring and doing seven-on-seven drills, like you do in college. They are more advanced than us. We only play eight games, so it was hard to get recruited as a quarterback."

The training he and his brothers completed with Demeris Johnson was key to his success, Dan believes.

"Demeris was a great motivator," he said. "We were blessed to find him out of nowhere, really. The guy really knows what he's doing. He pushed us to perform better in the off-season. If I didn't work out with him, I would have been so far behind on drills and form running, because all the other kids at college were already doing it."

Many college programs were interested in Dan but looked at his size and thought he would fit better as a lineman or tight end. Dan's stubborn streak, however, made him more determined to prove his ability under center.

"I don't know why he kept quarterback in his head," his father lamented years later. "He kept saying, 'Nope, I want to play QB.' After we visited Purdue, I told him, 'Dan you've got to change your mind here. It's not going to happen at QB.' He was a good quarterback in high school, but to do that at the college level, you have to be unbelievable. He just kept fighting it."

"He was stubborn and rightfully so," Mammoliti said. "He put so much time into it, I think he wanted to say, 'At least give me a shot.' He had a fantastic arm and his mechanics were good. But he got so big and was caught up in a time when the style of offenses was changing. The pocket-type quarterback was getting phased out, and the mobile kid who can run the spread option was coming into vogue."

"I wouldn't say I was stubborn about it," Dan contested. "That's not the right term. I'd call it relentless."

An early scholarship offer came from the University at Buffalo, just a few miles from his family home. But having watched Gordie experience success in Jacksonville, Dan wanted to travel out of state as well. Queries flooded his mailbox, but none contained an offer to play quarterback. Everyone envisioned him as a tight end or lineman. The University of Maryland, however, suggested an intriguing proposition.

"Maryland said they would bring him in as a quarterback and let his play tell them if he was a quarterback or not," his father summarized.

"They looked at me and had it in the back of their minds that I could play tight end," Dan admitted. "But they gave me a chance at quarterback. I was doing pretty well through spring ball, but finally decided I wanted to get on the field faster. They didn't push me into tight end, but left it up to me."

Making the position switch took some getting used to. But Dan was not afraid of hard work or learning new things.

"He never gave up," his father observed. "Dan had never had his hand down on the ground before. It was a whole new experience for him. He had never blocked or done any of that stuff. But he's more grounded than the other guys. He's a warrior in the weight room. He's always on time and always last to leave. He's doing anything he can to stay one step ahead of the next guy, you know? He doesn't have all the skills that Robbie does. For Robbie it comes natural, but Danny has to work at it constantly."

Seeing his older brother succeed was strong motivation for Rob, who is four years younger.

"He was the first one in our family to get a full scholarship, and that was huge," Rob explained. "He laid the baseline. I watched him play and saw what he did to get stronger. His work ethic motivated me."

After a redshirt year, Dan played in five games for the Maryland Terrapins in 2005, catching two passes for thirty-seven yards, including a twenty-five-yard touchdown. The following season, he played thirteen games, including nine starts, but was primarily a blocking tight end. He garnered an award that year for earning highest grade point average among his teammates. In 2007, Dan played eleven games, catching seven passes for sixty-six yards. He also received an award for public service.

During his senior year, 2008, Dan started twelve games and developed into more of a pass catcher. He snagged twenty-seven receptions for 287 yards, including three touchdowns. At season's end he was named an honorable mention All–Atlantic Coast Conference player.

Dan and his wife, the former Brittany Blujus, have dated since their senior year of high school. After spending semesters at Canisius and Buffalo State colleges, she transferred to Maryland so they could be closer together.

"He had this big binder of football plays, and he was always studying," she recalled. "It's a forty-five-minute flight from Baltimore to Buffalo, and when we flew home, he buried his head in that binder. He made index cards in a plastic filing system, and I used to quiz him. I had no idea what it meant, but I'd ask him to name a play, and flip the card over to see if he was right."

During his time at Maryland, his younger brother Chris joined the football team as a fullback but left after two seasons to play in Arizona.

"Chris went to Maryland with me," Dan said. "We always hung out and he was playing well. But they were playing another fullback, so Chris saw an opportunity somewhere else and took advantage of it."

Dan earned a marketing degree and continued to pursue an MBA after he graduated. He began the process to be nominated as a Rhodes Scholar but decided instead to concentrate on a football career.

"Probably my sophomore or junior year in college is when I started thinking about playing professionally," he said. "I began comparing myself to other guys and thought I could do it."

He entered the NFL draft in 2009. Predraft experts ranked him in impressive company: Draft Countdown assessed Dan as the twenty-first-best tight end prospect. The NFL Draft Scout ranked him eleventh out of ninety-six potential tight ends, projecting him as a fifth- or sixth-round selection. After intense training, he performed well at the NFL Scouting Combine, opening the eyes of many scouts.

Until that point, he was reluctant to admit that becoming a pro football player was his dream.

"People always asked what I wanted to be when I was older," he recalled. "You can't say you're going to be an athlete, because every kid in class wants to be a professional sports player, and I knew the chances are slim you're going to make it as a professional. So I'd try to think of something else to say. But throughout the years I knew in the back of my mind that's what I wanted to be. That was the dream I stuck with. I was a great athlete and I loved being a team player. I always tried to help other players get better along with me."

On April 26, 2009, day two of the annual NFL draft, the Gronkowskis hosted a huge party at their family home, expecting Dan's name to be called sometime that afternoon. The spacious family room was filled to the brim, with snacks and drinks and the big-screen TV flashing images of teams' selections. A local news station sent a camera crew to capture the excitement.

Dressed in a black polo shirt and black baseball cap turned backwards, his long hair flowing toward his shoulders, Dan waited to hear his fate. As the fifth and sixth rounds came and went, tensions grew. Dan alternately paced the room, walked alone in the backyard, and tossed basketballs at a net on the tennis court adjacent to the driveway, while frequently checking his cell phone.

Finally, nearing 7:00 P.M., with only two picks remaining in the seventh and final round, Dan received a call from the Detroit Lions. He had been selected with the 255th overall pick. Moments after he hung up, the Gronkowski family room exploded in excitement when Dan's name flashed on the TV screen. His brothers leaped up and chest-bumped him; Rob sprung up and down as if bouncing on an invisible pogo stick. Dan's father and mother calmly offered quotes to the news reporter.

"It took a while," Dan said that day. "But this is a dream come true. It doesn't matter where you get drafted. I'm ready to go to Detroit and get to work."

His rookie year in Detroit was a learning experience. The previous season, the Lions had become the NFL's first-ever 0-16 team, so there was plenty of room for improvement. But the roster was filled with young talent, including superstar receiver Calvin Johnson and quarterback Matthew Stafford. Dan spent much of the season jumping between the fifty-three-man squad and the practice roster. Promoted to the team when another tight end was injured, Dan caught one pass for four yards against the Baltimore Ravens. Later that week, he was cut and re-signed to the practice squad. Dan signed five different contracts that year — a separate form was required for each move up or down.

"Starting off in Detroit, I improved my route running a lot," Dan said. "I just worked at getting better. When I was there, they made so many moves. We had a new general manager and new coach. Every day they had someone new in and someone else gone. It was crazy. They brought in hardworking guys, winning guys, and tried to build up their defensive line."

Entering his second season, Dan faced stiff competition to earn a spot with the Lions again. Three tight ends were stacked above him on the depth chart.

"The worst scenario was that he would have gone back on the practice squad," Gordy said, recalling cutdown day in September 2010. "We were fairly sure if that happened he would be claimed by some other team, possibly the Jets or Bills. We were looking at who needed tight ends. When he got the call that said he'd been traded to Denver, it threw us all for a loop."

With the 4:00 P.M. cutdown looming, Dan was traded to the Denver Broncos for cornerback Alphonso Smith. It was a sudden and unexpected shift of fortune.

"Going to Denver was crazy," Dan recalled. "I arrived there and had to learn the whole offense in one week. It was totally different than the offense I had been in. I was at the facility from seven in the morning until nine at night. I really only had time to go home and sleep. Plus it's always hard to move to another place, because you have to figure out all the little things around you."

The crash course in offense was another challenge. Dan needed to know where tight ends lined up, what play was called, distances of each route, where to block on certain plays, who was helping block, and what calls might be made on the offensive line.

"It's a lot to process," Dan admitted. "Besides quarterback, tight end is the hardest position for knowing stuff. You have to be responsible for running, blocking, receiving, and fullback duties."

On opening weekend, the hard work paid dividends: Dan played twenty-five snaps in an offense he had not known eight days earlier. But adjusting to change was easier because of his work ethic.

"I always had an itch believing that I had to do more," Dan reflected. "Growing up, I'd try to get people to work out with me, but nobody ever wanted to do it. Am I just crazy? I know I need to do this to get in shape. I have this thing, I don't know where it's from, but the mental aspect pushes me past people. I always believed that I have to do this or that to get prepared and get my body ready."

As the season progressed, he played in twelve games, catching eight passes for sixty-five yards. Denver faced a three-headed quarterback controversy with Kyle Orton, Tim Tebow, and Brady Quinn. Head coach Josh McDaniels was fired in early December. With so much uncertainty surrounding the Broncos' future, Dan worried about his odds of remaining with the club for long.

When the 2010 season ended, Dan continued to work out but took a respite from the whirlwind of the Mile High City. The following July, he and Brittany married. Dan tweeted that the ceremony would be more extravagant than William and Kate's royal nuptials earlier that spring, joking that only two billion people watched the British wedding.

By August, it was back to Colorado for training camp. With a year of experience in the Broncos' organization, Dan hoped to settle into a routine but knew he was in another dogfight for a job.

"During the off-season, we got a new coach, Coach [John] Fox, who brought in his guys and drafted new guys," Dan said. "I got cut on the last day, and New England called my agent on Tuesday. I went out there, had a tryout, and signed with them."

Moving from a team in transition to a perennial powerhouse offered a huge upside. The added bonus was that Dan was now playing alongside his brother Rob, an emerging superstar who had made a name for himself in 2010.

Rob garnered a reputation for being a goofball, silly in and out of the locker room. Four years older, Dan is more serious and intense. Immediately their teammates noticed the difference.

"I thought it was going to be very interesting, like I was going to have two idiots right next to me on both sides," Patriots receiver Wes Welker joked to the media while sitting at his dressing stall. "But [Dan] is actually pretty bright. I was surprised."

After playing twenty-five snaps on opening night and starting in a three-tight-end formation in week two, Dan was cut before the third game with an injured hamstring. Being dismissed prevented him from a potential homecoming against the Buffalo Bills, a game in which Rob caught seven passes for 109 yards with two touchdowns.

Three weeks later, once his hamstring had recovered enough that he could play, Dan rejoined the team. But as the season progressed, injuries in other positions began to mount, and Dan was cut again after week nine to make room for new players who were signed to fill those voids.

"The first time I was hurt, so I needed to get healthy, then come back," he said. "The next time, the team had a lot of injuries, so that left me wondering how long it might take to get back. For a time, I thought I'd be back before the end of the year, because they kept my locker stall intact. If another team called, I'm sure my agent, Drew Rosenhaus, would call New England and they could figure something out."

Because of this uncertainty, fall 2011 was a difficult time for Dan. He existed week to week in blocks of limbo, unsure if the Patriots would be calling for his services again or if he should consider moving to another team. Doing that might lend greater job security, but he would surrender a legitimate chance to win a Super Bowl with his brother.

"So many changes definitely take an emotional toll on you, but you just have to keep fighting and take advantage of your chances. Hopefully you get another chance and get out there and fight."

When weeks stretched and New England did not re-sign Dan, he continued to look elsewhere for work. Several teams inquired about signing him—but not until after week seventeen. They wanted Dan to experience an entire off-season to learn their system. On December 23, Dan signed a two-year deal with the Cleveland Browns, hoping to land in a spot where he could stay for some time. He dressed for the final two games of the season but played sparingly as he learned another new offense.

Because of his gypsy ways, Dan viewed pro football with a wary eye, despite being only twenty-six years old. Superstars like his brother Rob have an entirely different experience with the business end of the game, where money and opportunity are un-rolled like a red carpet.

"There is a whole other side of football that a lot of people don't see," Dan mused, shaking his head and lowering his al-ready-deep voice. "It's crazy. You've got to get on a team and per-form, and hopefully they like you and you can stick for a while. There are so many guys that just go in for rookie camps and so many cuts being made. You really don't know what's going on behind the scenes."

Bouncing from team to team is challenging enough, but the moves also impact his wife. After graduating with a degree in elementary education in 2008, Brittany began teaching full-time in Maryland. They planned to maintain a long-distance relationship, but once Dan left for Detroit, his absence felt tangible. She claimed she wasn't fully "checked in" at her job. After waiting patiently through the day for his evening call, Brittany realized she would rather move to be with him. The various moves, after all, would be temporary.

"It would be different if we were older and had four kids," she said. "This is an opportunity that we're going to enjoy now. It's so exciting and thrilling. I can't explain to you how proud I feel when he runs onto the field to the cheers of the crowd. Any type of stress I'm feeling just goes away."

Still, moving to a new city is hard.

"My only connection to these different places is Dan's job," she said. "I've become a professional packer. I know exactly where the silicone wrap is at Lowe's. When he signs with a new team, I get really excited but try to stay calm so he doesn't have to worry."

Playing for four organizations has allowed Dan to witness the inner workings of the league in a way many players do not see.

"You definitely notice a difference in mindset by playing on different teams. You see how things work with the coaches and what type of players they bring in. New England brings in guys that are very businesslike. They want their people to be hardworking, put in the time, and know their stuff. If someone gets hurt at one position, another guy will fill in, because he's supposed to know it. You have to be able to do different stuff."

Several examples from the 2011 season were evident: backup wide receiver Julian Edelman spent significant time playing defensive back when injuries struck there. Deion Branch moved inside to play slot receiver when needed. Thanks to his leaping ability, Rob even joined the defense for one play at the end of a game. He was inserted as a defensive back, instructed to swat down the ball on a Hail Mary toss.

Each team has similarities as well. Most of the athletes he encountered are driven and passionate, willing to log long hours and extra time to achieve success, displaying the sort of extra work that Dan had always done.

"When you get higher in the professional ranks, those are the guys that were doing the same things as me, putting in the extra time," he said. "It's like that in the pros. In New England, everyone was at the practice facility early. That's normal."

As the 2011 season ended, Dan found a new home in Cleveland but not necessarily a new role. He had been a third-string tight end for the past three seasons, bouncing among teams. The Browns made no promises of a starting role. Dan was simply happy for another opportunity. He hoped to stick with the Browns and establish himself there.

He was cut from the roster before the 2012 season, but continued to train, hoping for a chance to land with another team.

"In college I was known for blocking," Dan said. "But when I got to Detroit I learned how to receive. My tight end coach was more of a receiving coach so I got better at that. When I went to Denver they looked at me as more of a receiving tight end. Sometimes I feel I'm stuck in the middle. I feel like I'm good at doing both things, but I want to be great at one. I'm looking at myself trying to pick one of these out. During the off-season I'm going to try to get bigger and concentrate on blocking. I weigh about two fifty-five, but tight ends that block are two seventy-five. That's what teams are looking for. Blocking was my strength in college. I've got to get back to that."

True to form, Dan met the challenge he had set for himself and gained fifteen pounds in the off-season, tipping the scales at 270. Dan's college coaches instilled in him the importance of drilling the guy in front of you. Dan hopes to return to that mentality as he forges ahead. Despite four moves in three years, he is not discouraged, nor is he ready to give up on football.

"I'm going to go as long as I can," he vowed. "At this point in my career I want to get on a team and stick for a few years. Right now I want to get better. Bigger, stronger, faster. I improve every year. I might not be the best player on the team, but I've won so many most-improved-player awards. I'm going to keep working hard and improving until my body gets older and I can't go anymore."

Although he is the second-oldest brother, Dan was the first to excel at football. Everyone in the family agrees that his success opened the door for Chris, Rob, and Goose.

The brothers welcome young Goose into the world. From left, Rob (with a black eye), Chris (holding Goose), Dan, and Gordie.

Outside the right-field gates at Baltimore Orioles ballpark, 1995. From left, Dan, Gordy (holding Goose), Rob, Diane, Gordie, Chris.

7

Competition and Physical Play

"What we do now as professional athletes is what we did
when we were kids running out of control."

— DAN GRONKOWSKI

WHY ARE THE GRONKOWSKIS so successful as athletes?

What happened under that roof to defy the long odds
of making it to the highest level of sports? Aside from astronom-
ical food bills, with two refrigerators and two freezers stocked at
all times, was it just good genes? Motivating parents? Something
in the water?

Often athletes use sport as a way to escape the squalor of a
poor home life. The game provides a focus that is different from
the poverty that defines every day. That is not the case with the
Gronkowskis. They are an upper-class family from a wealthy
suburb, educated and financially stable. There was no plight
from which to escape, no need for sports to provide a better life.

Why, then, are the Gronkowskis successful where others aren't?

There is no easy answer, only contributing factors.

"Looking back at the things I do and where I am now, that's because we always used to be so competitive," Dan Gronkowski said. "I don't think many kids did the things we did. We had tournaments and fought over who won games. We brought a competitive side to everything. We were hitting and checking each other all the time. That was our normal, running into each other."

The eldest brother, Gordie, agreed that competition defined their early years.

"Who wouldn't want five athletic brothers, all close to each other in age?" Gordie wondered rhetorically. "We were like a team out there. We'd play two-on-two hoops, two-on-two mini-stick hockey, two-on-two roller hockey against each other. We made up games and had competitions in the backyard. Even though it was fun, there was always that competition. Everyone wanted to be better than the other person. Things used to get heated. Rob used to throw his mini-stick at everyone. Golf clubs would get chucked. It didn't matter what the sport was, we were always competitive."

"What we do now as professional athletes is what we did when we were kids running out of control," Dan said. "Not many people have four other brothers where they can always have a pickup game. There were times we were watching TV and someone would say, 'Let's go in the basement and get a game going.' And next thing you know, there's a competition. Anytime we went in the backyard, we had a ready-made team of two on two."

So competition was a contributing factor. But so were collisions and contact, well beyond the typical "boys will be boys" roughhousing that characterizes many kids' play. Often the physical toll was punishing, and sometimes it was by choice.

"Chris would beat the hell out of Rob," their father explained. Gordy recalled regular fights between them as kids, suggesting Rob reveled in the conflict.

"Robbie would never give up. One day Chris beat him up, and then Rob waited until Chris was sleeping on the couch, snuck over, and wailed him in the face, just to get even. He didn't care. Chris leaped up and beat the living shit out of him again. Rob would crawl out and say something stupid again and get the crap knocked out of him a third time. It was weird that he loved that, but the kid never backed down. He just kept coming and coming."

The physical punishment may be a contributing factor to Rob's fearlessness on the football field. His speed makes it difficult for defenders to catch him, but once contact is made, it usually takes more than one person to tackle Rob.

"That's why he's one of the best tight ends in the game now, because the kid has no fear," Gordy said.

Fearlessness aside, Rob is a Pro Bowl tight end who plays with the joy of a child, as evident in his signature move after scoring a touchdown, when Rob surveys a spot of end-zone turf and winds up, windmill fashion, spiking the ball into the ground with power and ferocity—Gronking it. Anything beneath that ball would be crushed. In fact, after his second season, Rob was invited to a Worcester Sharks minor-league hockey game, where he led the ceremonial puck drop. But instead of following tradition and merely releasing the puck, letting it fall to the ice, Rob stood and eyed the faceoff dot. Stepping back, he wound up and Gronked it.

The audience erupted in applause when the rubber disk split in two.

When it came to competition on the home front, it wasn't always Gronkowskis versus Gronkowskis. Occasionally the brothers would band together to form a team against neighbors or friends. Those kids didn't stand a chance.

"Sometimes it would be the group of brothers against everyone else," Gordie recalled with a smile. "It wouldn't matter, as long as we were playing. Sometimes we were poor sports. If we were snowmobiling or four-wheeling, sometimes we raced to the point where it was dangerous."

By all accounts, Rob's behavior was the most reckless. In addition to reveling in physical punishment, he had a wild streak and sometimes displayed poor judgment.

"One time, we were racing four-wheelers," Gordie recalled. "Rob had his going forty miles an hour and lost the edge, turning directly into a tree. He totaled the brand-new machine and wrapped his knee around the trunk. We tied up the four-wheeler and brought it back, thankful that he wasn't seriously hurt. Luckily, he wore a helmet. We never told our parents what happened and they didn't notice the crumpled bike. Three or four weeks later, we realized Rob was wearing sweatpants all the time."

His father's nickname for Robbie was "Slobbie," so Rob's fashion choices weren't exactly a topic of household conversation. Still, the brothers noticed the sweats and wondered what was up.

"Turns out a tree branch went through the skin, and he had a huge chunk of wood embedded in his leg," Gordie recalled. "The skin healed over it. He went to a specialist, and they cut it open and pulled out a sliver as thick as your finger. His leg was pussed all over and he was hurting the whole time but didn't say anything. It shows you how tough the kid is. That's the extent to which we take things. It gets dangerous because we want to win a backyard race on a four-wheeler."

Because of the brothers' size, sometimes the physical play had to be stifled. Getting the big kid angry was never a good idea.

"In high school, Rob was a boy in a man's body," commented Bill Gorman, the assistant basketball coach at Williamsville North High School, where Rob played on the varsity team for three years, beginning as a ninth grader. "He's freakishly strong and he lives for contact. If somebody tried to knock him around, that wasn't going to happen."

Part of Gorman's duties as assistant coach was to keep an eye on Rob. Because of his stature, other teams would often use several players to cover him, bumping and jostling to distract Rob from his game.

"He wouldn't get calls against him because he was so big," said longtime friend Charlie Teal. "Rob never got the benefit of the doubt on any fouls. Referees figured he should be able to deal with it."

"I was the two guard," explained John Ticco, a high school teammate. "I'd get the ball, dump it to Rob, and my guy would leave me and go down and hack him. He got fouled so much. They weren't touch fouls, they were hack fouls. We nearly got into a brawl once because the other team kept cheap-shotting him up high when he'd go up to dunk. It got to a point where it was dangerous for Rob to be playing the game."

"If his fuse got short, he might seriously hurt someone," Gorman recalled. "He could play rough, but because he was so big, it looked worse than he intended. There were times when he'd say, 'I'm going to kill that kid,' and he literally could have. We'd get him off the floor, give him a little breather with a sub, and get him calmed down."

"Coach, they're hitting me," Rob would complain.

"Take it easy," Gorman said. "You're fine." Only when he returned to an even temper would Rob be reinserted into the game.

All the Gronkowski brothers had large frames, and added muscle when they began working out at age fourteen. But Gordie, Dan, Chris, and Goose didn't completely fill out until their late teens. During his redshirt year playing baseball at Jacksonville University, for instance, eighteen-year-old Gordie grew from six feet three to six six, and added thirty pounds to his frame. Rob, however, was big and muscular at a younger age.

"I saw them all play in high school," said Glenn Gronkowski, Gordy's brother and the boys' uncle. "What's freaky is how they grew. They weren't as big as they are now until they got into the senior high and got older. All of a sudden they had unbelievable growth spurts."

The brothers were smart enough to use their size as an advantage. In addition, each possessed a resolve to achieve.

Gorman recalled a high school basketball game where Rob was being double-teamed with a boy in front and another behind him, limiting Rob's access to the ball. Frustration grew on the part of the Williamsville North team, which was losing because its best player was being denied. During a time-out Rob approached his coaches at the bench, shaking his head.

"Have our point guard throw the ball high and I'll get it," Rob promised.

This was not a play they had practiced before, but the coaches figured they were losing already. Something needed to change. In the worst-case scenario, they would lose by more points if Rob's idea didn't work.

"Three plays in a row, we came down, threw it high, literally a foot over the rim, and Robbie went and got it each time," Gorman said. "Two of them were baskets. We ended up winning the game because of that strategy."

During a later time-out, Rob trotted to the bench and grinned knowingly at his coaches. "I told you I'd get it."

Rob's physical dominance was evident from a young age. By fourteen, his frame was already like a bodybuilder's.

"It was embarrassing when he took his shirt off, because he was so cut," recalled Chuck Swierski, the varsity basketball coach at Williamsville North High School. "Watching him in high school, he was so much bigger, so much stronger, so much faster than everybody else."

His uncle Glenn remembered seeing a basketball game that opened his eyes to how impressive an athlete Rob had become as a high school sophomore.

"I saw him play where the guard threw a lob pass from close

to half court," Glenn said. "Rob went up with a big guy in front of him, jumped over the guy, grabbed the ball, and jammed it through the hoop with two hands. I remember thinking, 'This kid's got some serious ability.' It blew me away, really."

At times, Rob's strength could be overwhelming. Gorman compared Rob's physical traits to those of Lennie, the character in John Steinbeck's novel *Of Mice and Men*. Gorman is quick to point out that the similarities don't extend beyond the physical—Rob doesn't need to be told what to do—but like Lennie, Rob doesn't know his own strength.

Sometimes the physical play led to unintended consequences.

"During exam week our gym wasn't available because all the desks were set up for tests, so we had to run practice at Williamsville East," Swierski said. The district is large enough that it contains three high schools. The intradistrict rivalry can be intense.

"We were doing a lay-up drill." Swierski recalled. "Rob caught the ball on the baseline, went up and dunked it, and didn't hang on the rim but shattered the backboard and came down with the rim in his hands. He just went up strong and the backboard completely shattered. Williamsville East wasn't happy. It kind of screwed up their season for a few weeks because it took them a while to get a new one. They didn't have a backup anywhere, and by the time they ordered it and had it installed, they had to move a few games around. They thought we did it on purpose because of the whole school-rivalry thing, but he honestly didn't. The kid is just that strong."

• • •

As a stay-at-home mom raising five active boys, Diane Gronkowski's duties were far more demanding than any nine-to-five office job.

"I pretty much woke up, turned on the ovens, and started cooking," she said with a laugh. "I liked to cook and grocery shop, so it was okay with me. If I wasn't driving one of them somewhere, that's what I was doing. People used to ask me if I was grocery shopping for a group home. You could say that."

The family often bought half a cow, or several forty-pound boxes of poultry. In addition to the refrigerator in the kitchen, there was a second refrigerator in the garage, accompanied by two full-size freezers. None contained leftovers, only supplies for the next meal.

"There were never any leftovers," she said. "They ate, I'll tell you that. While I was doing dishes, the boys would come back and pick at the dinner we just had. I never put food away. They were never full."

The boys would regularly wander into the kitchen and ask what was around to eat. A favorite phrase was "But Mom, I'm starving."

"We just finished eating, and a half hour later, they said they were starving," Diane recalled. "We did not eat out. There was no McDonald's or Burger King or pizza night. Every meal was homemade. One reason was nutrition. Another was the expense. Can you imagine how much it would cost to get these guys full? Another big reason was that we rarely ate at the same time. Everyone had a different schedule. One summer I had thirteen baseball teams going at once. There were house teams, select teams, travel teams, and there were five boys. So how could you possibly eat at the same time?"

The Gronkowski home was a familiar stop for the boys' friends. It was the place where kids gathered, and Diane made sure that everyone was welcome.

She invited kids inside, baked cookies, asked them to stay for dinner, not worrying about little things like dirty shoes. Sometimes a boy would stay for an extended time if his parents moved away or got divorced. The welcome mat was always on display. Diane was the lone female in a male-dominated house.

"I was outnumbered," she admitted with a laugh. "At times it was frustrating. It was always the guys' point of view. Nobody ever looked at things from my perspective. There was a male dog and we had a goldfish for eleven years. I was convinced he was male, too, because there was nothing in the house that wasn't."

To illustrate the point, Diane recalled that her sons often fell asleep in bedrooms other than their own. Whenever they were tired, they would simply spread out in a bed, regardless of whether it was that boy's room.

"More than once I woke up the wrong kid," she explained. "Everyone just slept where they wanted to sleep that night."

Diane was always organized. Having to balance the schedules of five boys, often the majority of her day was spent driving kids to practices and being sure their homework was done in the limited time between sports.

"There were Saturdays when one had hockey at four fifty in the morning and another had hockey at nine o'clock in Niagara Falls and a third had hockey at two in the Pepsi Center and then there was another game at eight that night at Sabreland," she said, mentioning rinks that are several towns apart. "So when we went to bed the night before, all the hockey gear was loaded into the van. You didn't wait until it was time to leave to decide you needed your skates sharpened or your equipment washed. The van had to be full of gas because you're not going to be driving the next morning low on gas. I also worried about what we were having for dinner, because I was going to be gone all day. Dinner was made the night before."

Those organizational skills, Diane believes, have rubbed off onto her children. Despite their active lifestyles, the boys are able to juggle different responsibilities. But she is more proud of the fact that her sons are good people.

"Yes, three of them are professional football players, but that doesn't last forever," she said. "They have to have something else behind that. They've worked hard for what they have, but the whole world isn't sports. I always tried to teach them right from wrong. I sent them to religion class to learn morals. Trying to get them to treat others the way they wanted to be treated was important."

When each boy left for college, Diane explained that he had been given opportunities that others may not have.

"I filled out all the paperwork, made sure they had their physicals on time, drove them to and from every practice, checked that their homework was done. I gave my twenty-four/seven to them. I'm proud that they're all good citizens, athletic, and have done well academically. If you can get one person in your family to achieve that, it's phenomenal. But we have five of them who achieved. It was definitely worth it."

• • •

"I could never have done it without her," Gordy reflected. "I'm not taking all the credit. She was a great mom who worked hard to get them to the next level. She got those boys through school. Danny and Chris were easy, but she sat at that table every night with Gordie making sure his homework was done and that it was done right. She spent hours running them around each day, and was always there to defend her kids."

Once, when Gordy was coaching his boys' hockey team, he was out of town during a scheduled practice. The team's other coach could not attend either, so Diane laced up her skates and ran practice in their place.

"It probably wasn't the best practice they ever had," Gordy said with a laugh. "But we couldn't be there, so she was."

Although they are no longer married, he is quick to point out her contribution to raising their boys. She was the one who cooked healthy meals. She was the one who ran them to and from endless practices and games. She made sure their paperwork was complete, their education was stressed, and that schedules were kept.

"She did an awesome job of managing us," Rob said. "Without her contributions, we wouldn't have had the great childhood that we did."

"I give her all the credit for that," Gordy noted. "My role was to oversee them in sports."

All the brothers were coached by their father. The training was far more nurturing than has sometimes been portrayed in the media. One report implied that Gordy took his sons to the backyard when they were four years old and whipped tennis balls at their heads. In fact, he did lob tennis balls toward them, but it was to build hand-eye coordination, not as punishment.

"When we were younger, my dad stressed that sports was all about having fun," Dan said.

Gordy coached travel baseball and youth hockey teams, largely so he could work with his sons, usually between the ages of eight and sixteen. As his business grew, he tried to coach less but found it difficult to step away.

"As much as I wanted to get away from coaching, I never could," Gordy lamented, although since his boys have grown, there is a feeling of nostalgia surrounding those years. "I didn't always want to coach, but having boys forced me into it."

"He was so good at getting players on a team to become best friends," Dan said. "It didn't matter how big a dork the kid was or how popular or good an athlete he was. He got all the team-mates to be best friends. You don't see that too often. Most Little League teams just go out there. You're buddies with some guys on the team, but not everyone gels. In the house teams, my dad's plan was that everyone needed to get better. He'd start a kid for a couple innings, and if the kid was doing well, he'd keep pitching. If not, he'd put me in the lineup. The kids who played Little League with us will say their best year was when Mr. G was the coach. He made it fun for everybody."

Always the tireless worker, Gordy put in long hours studying coaching techniques and watching videos of other teams. He made up cards as a reward for players who achieved something special. Gordy knew the focus of the game should be about kids, not adults.

"We were blessed to have good coaches and good people around who had the best interests at heart for the kids," Dan recalled. "When parents at games are yelling at kids all the time, it becomes about them, and that takes away from the kids. The teams I played on, you didn't see much of that."

Gordy knew that the young people he coached needed to feel a bond with one another. So, too, did their parents. Another key to his success was to get fellow parents involved.

"We were a real team made up of good friends," Dan recalled. "And he developed the kids. He wouldn't just put the best player in to pitch the whole game. Kids that weren't so good would play, so they got better. By the end of the season, all the kids who weren't very good when they started became pretty decent. We'd go right to the playoffs. One year we won the championship eighteen to one because we were so far ahead of anyone else."

The picture wasn't always rosy, but Gordy stressed that setbacks are a natural part of life.

"All my kids griped and bitched at some point," he said. "When Gordie was in a batting slump at college, I was afraid to take his call. He'd complain that he hated the game and that everything was BS. I always taught my kids that there are going to be bumps in the road. It's never an easy path. But the one who comes out in the end is the one who knows how to handle the bumps. You just have to keep battling through."

A decade removed from having his father as a coach, Dan still speaks with pride about Gordy's accomplishments. There remains something special about his youth and the time his dad spent nurturing him and his brothers and other kids in the community.

"We won with every single team he coached in Little League. My dad had all these systems he used. In hockey, it was a different story. We'd always go to the championship but we'd never win." Dan paused, then let out a deep laugh. "I think he knew more about baseball."

Chris as a high school baseball star, 2004.

During his rookie season in 2010, Chris played fullback for the Dallas Cowboys.

8

Chris: Brains and a Pedigree

"One day, when they were at college, Rob told me Chris actually studied that day. It lasted for ten minutes. But still, he always got straight As."

— GORDY GRONKOWSKI

IN SPRING 2012, NEARLY seven years after graduating from high school, Chris Gronkowski realized a dream by attending an Ivy League college. As part of an NFL-sponsored program on business management and entrepreneurship, Chris was one of thirty pro football players to attend Harvard University for an intense one-week course.

"It's a business class for players," he explained. "It teaches economics and helps guys make decisions about investments. You look at financial records of businesses and actual case studies. You ask yourself, is this a good investment? We dealt with real estate deals and how to handle negotiations."

Many NFL players invest in businesses, both during their careers and when their playing days end, so the league is trying to

a foundation for them to make wise choices as they con-
ure careers and financial planning.

The middle child, Chris is smaller than the other Gronkowski
brothers. "Small" is a relative term. With a shock of blond hair
above the center of his forehead, Chris stands at six feet two
inches and weighs 245 pounds. His barrel chest and biceps
strain the fabric of his shirts. Compared to most of society, he
is a physical specimen. Next to his brothers, he gives up several
inches in height, but his chest and muscles are just as wide.

Chris has been dubbed the quiet son, the smartest in a clan of
smart kids. Family friends describe him as the toughest brother.
He was a high school athlete, playing football, hockey, and baseball. But he was also a high-honor-roll student who was accepted into the elite University of Pennsylvania to study business
in 2005. It was only an eleventh-hour offer to attend the University of Maryland on a football scholarship that twisted his life in
a different direction.

"I was all set to go to [Penn's] Wharton School," Chris explained. "At the last minute, Maryland called and offered me a
football scholarship. Some of the guys they originally offered
scholarships to didn't have high-enough grades. I was a little
smaller than many college recruits, so I wasn't getting many offers to play football."

Attending Maryland instead of the University of Pennsylvania was not a decision that kept Chris up at night. He immediately accepted the scholarship and the chance to play alongside
his older brother Dan.

"The Ivy League doesn't offer scholarships, so I would have
been on the hook for more than forty grand per year at Penn,"

he said. "True, you're going to have great opportunities after graduation, but that's a lot of money to pay back."

Chris smiled as he told the story. There are benefits to being a smart guy.

"My teachers always said that having good grades was your ticket to success, and they were right," Chris admitted. "High grades were pretty much my ticket in. Plus, Dan was doing well at Maryland. He built a good reputation for our family."

Chris is the first to admit that those two things — brains and his family pedigree — have opened doors for him. On two separate occasions, college coaches figured that if one Gronkowski was good, another brother might be just as good. That logic paved the way to Chris's NFL career as well.

The third son, born at the end of 1986, Chris is two years younger than Dan and two years older than Rob. When he was a sophomore in high school, Dan was a senior, so they played varsity football together. Likewise, when Chris was a high school senior, Rob was a sophomore, so this time Chris was a teammate with his younger brother.

"One of the big things for us was pride," Chris explained. "When I played with Rob, I used to go all out so that when we got back to the huddle, I could say, 'Hey, Bro, did you see what I just did?' We would watch film together and I'd say, 'Look at me here.' We'd block together and take guys out and drill them. Part of the motivation was to impress your brother."

Mike Mammoliti, Williamsville North's varsity football coach, oversaw development of the Gronkowski brothers. Chris played fullback on offense and linebacker on defense.

"Chris was a little quieter early on. It was tough to get him to say a whole lot. He and another guy were the best players on our [junior varsity] squad. About six games into the season, they were so dominant on JV and we needed their help. We brought them both up with a couple games left in their freshman year. Then Chris started the next three years for us."

Despite his reserved manner, Chris was a versatile athlete who performed well on the field, according to the coach.

"Every once in a while he'd say something funny that caught you off-guard. He always came into my office after phys ed class and ate my food. As he got older, he became more vocal and wasn't as introverted. He blossomed into the person he became. He has a great sense of humor."

Gordy agreed that Chris was the quiet brother. Although all his boys are smart, Chris's brains set him apart.

"When it comes to academics, he's like an Einstein," Gordy said. "He doesn't put much effort into it. He's scary smart. I coached him in hockey when he was a kid, and he'd drive me nuts because he couldn't look me in the eyes. I'd be talking and he'd skate around looking all over. One day I got pissed and yelled at him."

"I heard you," Chris replied and repeated his father's instructions verbatim.

"It was scary and freaky," Gordy admitted. "He had straight As all through high school. Academics always came easy to him. But he's got a mean streak. He and Robbie used to beat the hell out of one another. If he gets mad, watch out."

At the University of Maryland, Chris redshirted his first year, then played the following two seasons. Another fullback, younger than Chris, received most of the reps with the first-team offense. Chris recognized this trend was going to continue, believing it was unlikely he would take the field. He began to consider another college.

By this time, Rob was one of the top recruits in the nation. Rob committed to attend the University of Arizona, and Chris saw an opportunity.

"The way it was going at Maryland, coaches were willing to do anything to put the other fullback in," Chris said. "Rob was such a big name that wherever he went, they were able to bring me in and give me a chance."

Coincidentally, Arizona had shown interest in Chris when he was a high school senior. He had talked with both the football and baseball teams about playing there. Rob had accompanied his older brother during a campus visit, which is how he became interested in the college. As a high school senior on campus, Chris viewed his game films with head football coach Mike Stoops.

"Coach Stoops told my dad I didn't have the speed or talent to play for them," Chris said with a laugh. Three years later, with Rob committed to Arizona, it was a different story.

As a transfer student, NCAA rules forced Chris to sit out one season of football when he moved to Arizona. But Chris wanted to stay active, so he tried out for the baseball team. He had not played organized baseball since his senior year of high school. The layoff didn't matter—Chris's talent was obvious.

"Chris was the best baseball hitter I've ever seen, period," said John Ticco, a family friend who played high school ball with both Rob and Chris and later played college baseball at Miami

University in Ohio. "I've seen a ton of players, but he's the best pure hitter I've seen. He could have gotten drafted out of high school, but he committed to football instead."

Harry Shaughnessy, a former professional player and long-time Western New York baseball coach, agreed. Shaughnessy coached all the brothers from the time they were in Little League and as they progressed through high school. He is close enough to the Gronkowski family that the boys jokingly refer to him as Uncle Harry.

"I've been around baseball my whole life," Shaughnessy said. "I stand by the statement that Chris is one of the best hitters I've ever seen. He could turn his wrists and cut on a fastball like nobody else. It was to the point where I was worried when my own son played third base when Chris was batting. I knew he loved football, but I told Gordy not to let the kid give up on baseball. I was convinced he could have a major-league career as a designated hitter."

Ticco admires and remains envious of Chris's natural talent.

"I worked my tail off all winter to come into baseball season and get my swing right," he recalled. "Chris played football and didn't do any baseball training in the winter. He just did his normal workouts. In the spring, he'd come to the first practice and pick up a bat."

"This is the first time I've held one of these since last year," Chris would say, taking a few practice swings at the air.

"When the pitch came, he'd kill it," Ticco said. "He'd blast it. It was crazy. To show how good he is, at Arizona he walked onto the number-one-ranked baseball team in the country."

Chris is humble when explaining the months he spent playing college baseball. The way he tells it, the requirements of two sports overwhelmed him.

"I was getting back into baseball," he said. "I had taken two years off, but came back, worked hard, and was killing it at first. But then I started doing football workouts and went to baseball workouts after that. This was every day. I was shot from the workouts. I was shedding weight. I lost twenty pounds and had no power anymore. I went from crushing it to struggling in both sports. It became a mess."

Chris finally approached the baseball coach, Andy Lopez, and initiated a candid discussion about his future. He thought it would be best to give up baseball and put his efforts exclusively into football.

"I told the coach that I'm on a scholarship for football, and he understood," Chris said. "I was glad to focus on just one sport."

Despite the shift, there was no guarantee that football would pan out.

"Coming to Arizona was a bit of a risk, because they hardly ever used a fullback," Chris said. "I thought I might get ten snaps a game if I got the starting job. I tried playing linebacker for a while, and that was fun because I got to go against Rob in practice."

The sibling rivalry was strong, but the boyhood days of Chris beating up Rob were over. In fact, the two lived together at Arizona, getting along like best friends.

"One day, when they were at college, Rob told me Chris actually studied that day," their father said, shaking his head. "It lasted for ten minutes. But still, he always got straight As. It was so funny because growing up, Rob and Chris couldn't stand each other, but then Chris went to Arizona to be with him and they ended up rooming together. Go figure."

Bragging rights were still part of the brotherhood, however.

"I played on the scout team when I first started at Arizona," Chris explained. "I was a linebacker during practice and I was all hyped up. Rob was running an out route and I was covering him. When he juked in, he was off-balance, so I threw him on the ground. He's lying there, and I'm slapping everyone up, bragging about my hit."

The receivers' coach, however, was not amused that his star tight end had been mistreated. He stormed onto the field, cursing Chris.

"You don't touch him like that!" the coach shouted. "Who do you think you are? You won't be on this team anymore if you do that again! You're a goddamn nobody!"

"What are you talking about?" Chris asked. "I'm his brother."

Suddenly, silence reigned.

"That coach didn't know what to do afterward," Chris recalled, laughing. "He had no clue what to say. He thought I was just some walk-on. It was awesome."

It didn't take Chris long to work his way into the lineup. He gave up defensive duties and focused on playing fullback. In his first game, he scored a touchdown. That and his impressive blocking opened the coaches' eyes to his potential. Suddenly, Chris's number was being called more often.

"I felt I was a better offensive player anyway," he said, explaining the position switch. "Once I got on the field, it started blowing up. I went from playing ten snaps a game to playing a majority of snaps by the end of the year. They brought Rob and me in at the same time. Mostly I was a fullback, but there were times I'd line up next to him as a wing, and we'd block the same guy. Or I would line up as a second tight end, and we would each run a streak down the middle to split the defense. The safety in the center had to choose which of us to cover."

Being the star, coverage often diverted to Rob. That opened opportunities for Chris. In his junior year, Chris caught eight balls for 198 yards.

"Every time I caught the ball, it was for a big gain," he said. "I caught a touchdown in a bowl game on national TV against BYU [Brigham Young University]. That touchdown put the game away. It was nice because it put me on some highlight shows and then everything opened up for me."

Despite their battles throughout childhood, Rob understood how tough his brother was.

"When I watched him on the field in high school and college, he inspired me to get my blocks down," Rob said. "He brought toughness to the table. Playing college football with him was an honor. We definitely helped each other out. It was great that every time he caught a pass, it was for a huge gain."

Around this time, Chris watched his older brother Dan get drafted by the Detroit Lions. He wondered if he could follow in those footsteps.

"During my junior year, I thought I might have a shot at the pros," he said. "Rob and I were watching game film, and he said, 'Those are some NFL blocks right there.' That's probably the first time I thought seriously about the NFL. I had to get over the fact that when you're growing up, people tell you the odds against making it. There are so many guys who are good players but don't get a shot. Once Dan did it, I knew I had a chance as well."

Chris attended the NFL's pro day but was disappointed there was little opportunity to catch passes and showcase his athletic ability. Instead, players were timed for speed. But because the event was held on turf, one-tenth of a second was added to the fastest times, with the premise that turf is a quicker surface than grass.

"I was with a bunch of other guys and performed pretty well, but I didn't feel like I made the impression I wanted to," Chris admitted. "Afterward, my agent said I had to go back and run on grass to prove those times I was clocked at weren't accurate."

Being Rob's brother provided Chris with another opportunity to perform in front of scouts. Coming off back surgery in spring 2010, Rob had not recovered enough to attend the NFL Scouting Combine. Once he regained his strength, a private pro day was held at Arizona for interested scouts. Rob was the featured athlete, but Chris attended too. This allowed him to be given a second look by pro teams.

"Everyone expects me to be good, because I'm a Gronkowski," Chris said. "Having my last name definitely helps."

After Chris's impressive showing alongside Rob, some draft experts predicted he might be selected as high as the fourth round. But fullback is a luxury position in today's NFL. Few teams keep a pure fullback on their roster. Often, a big running back or a tight end lines up to block for the featured runner.

"My agent knew my chances of getting drafted were pretty small," Chris admitted. "Teams were calling during the draft, but only one or two fullbacks were even picked that year. It wasn't a huge deal. Two minutes after the draft ended, I had the option to sign with Dallas. It looked like a good situation. At that point, I started cheering."

Attending the first practice, Chris was shocked to see Phil Costa, a former Maryland teammate and free-agent offensive lineman, playing center. The two had roomed together in college.

"It was kind of crazy when we walked into Dallas," Costa recalled. "Our lockers were right next to each other, and we became roommates again. We were both in the same boat, free agents trying to make the team. We didn't plan any of that. So it's really a small world."

Chris and his college pal instantly bonded again, trying to motivate each other, just like they had at Maryland.

"Phil and I knew how tough it would be to make the final roster," Chris noted. "From that first day we got there, we both said we were going to beat the odds no matter what it took."

The two trained together and ate together. Then ate again. And again.

"Every day we went in and played as hard as we could," Chris said. "We both had to put weight on, so we were in the weight room trying to pump each other up. We would work as hard as we could, then go home and shove food into our faces. It was to the point where we just about threw up every night."

"We cooked chicken and whole wheat pasta and brown rice," Costa explained. "We were both trying to add five to ten pounds. A lot of time, the last few bites of the meal we gagged trying to put it down."

Any free agent entering training camp has odds stacked against him. During August practices under the sweltering Texas sun, Chris impressed the Cowboys' coaches. Still, despite a strong training camp, he was nervous as cutdown day approached. Another fullback, Deon Anderson, had been a sixth-round draft pick in 2007, and few teams retained two players at that position.

"On cutdown day, they sat us in a room and kept pointing to guys who were cut," Chris said. "I was crouching behind people, trying to hide, thinking, 'Don't point at me.' I was pretty sure I was going to make it, but Dallas never kept two fullbacks before."

Anderson was the starter, but Chris earned a roster spot as his backup. But Anderson went down with an injury in the season opener. So in just his second week as a pro, Chris was moved into the starting lineup. He scored a touchdown, raising his profile.

"After that, they let Anderson go, so I was the only fullback left," Chris said.

It was a rags-to-riches story, something Hollywood might concoct. Chris, the low-profile Gronkowski brother, never as big a name as Dan or Rob, had defied long odds and become an NFL starter on a team that many experts considered a Super Bowl contender when the season began.

But the Cowboys began poorly. Entering a Monday-night game on October 25, their record was a lowly 1-4. Facing a must-win matchup against the New York Giants, star quarterback Tony Romo dropped back to pass and was tackled by Michael Boley. Although the pass was completed, Romo's shoulder was driven into the ground, where he laid on his back, reluctant to get up. As Romo was helped off the field, it appeared the bottom was dropping out of the Cowboys' season.

The media blamed a young fullback. Chris had missed a block.

"It was a play where anything could have happened," Chris said. "They had a delayed blitz. We had watched film all week and the Giants never once blitzed from that position. When the ball was snapped, I checked my guy. Coaches taught us to get into our route quickly, so I got out and this guy came late. Romo wound up and threw a long pass."

It became a defining moment in Chris's young career.

In the time that followed, Gordy was quick to defend his son. It was a simple missed block, he pointed out, that led to a bad result.

"That one frigging play," Gordy said, shaking his head. "I watched a Dallas game a year later and the announcers were still talking about it, blaming Chris. Give the kid a break."

Romo's injury forced him from the lineup. As the season progressed and losses accumulated, head coach Wade Phillips was replaced by Jason Garrett. Cracks were already evident in the armor, but Romo's injury became a touchstone. Chris took the heat.

"I was crucified for that missed block," he said. "It was crazy. They still talk about it. The media in Dallas is tough. You have to deal with them trying to tear you down. Defenses blitz to hit the quarterback. It's something that happens every game. The bad thing is he got hurt."

Chris addressed the missed block immediately after the game.

"I told Tony I was sorry and that I made a mistake," he said. "He said that's what happens in football, and I should keep working hard. He didn't blame me. He's a true leader and a team player. Guys understand that people make mistakes."

Despite the media attention, teammates did not resent Chris. Football players understand that injuries are fluky, part of the game.

"Everybody's out there trying to do their best," said Costa, Chris's roommate and fellow rookie at the time. "Guys in the locker room understand that. It just so happens Tony got hurt on the play, which magnifies the mistake a hundred times. That happens a lot in the NFL, where a guy will miss an assignment. When someone doesn't get hurt, it's just another play. But Tony did get hurt, and there's the difference."

With backup quarterback Jon Kitna leading the Dallas offense, the Cowboys fought their way from a 1-5 record to 6-10 by season's end. But a shadow still hung over Chris because of the negative publicity around Romo's injury.

He entered 2011 hoping for a shot at redemption. Chris wanted to wipe away everyone's memory of a single play and prove that he was a complete player. After a long training camp, he was among the final cuts. Despite the surprise, Chris wasn't unemployed for long.

"During the last cuts I was let go by Dallas," he said. "The Indianapolis Colts called the next day. I had to go through waivers, and the team with the fewest wins the year before got the first claim. My agent told me that two other teams tried to claim me. But of the three, the Colts had the worst record, which is funny because they won ten games the year before. I received a call from the Colts at noon and two hours later I was on a plane heading for Indianapolis."

Without quarterback Peyton Manning, who missed the entire season due to a neck injury, the Colts' season started in free fall and continued downhill. Chris played in seven games until he was injured on a special-teams play against New Orleans.

"I was running full speed and a guy came to block me," Chris explained. "I shed the block, reached out, and tackled Darren Sproles. I didn't get him clean, but almost clotheslined him. Doing that, I pulled my arm back and tore the tendon, ripping it right off the shoulder. The tackle was made, but I knew immediately that something was wrong."

With a torn pectoralis major, Chris underwent surgery to reattach the muscle to the shoulder and bone. It was a similar procedure to the one his father had endured as a college football player. Chris was placed on injured reserve, ending his season.

Being injured is a challenge for any athlete. Technically, Chris was a member of the team, but he did not practice with the guys, instead spending five days each week at rehab and attending games on Sunday.

"It was the first time I hadn't played because of an injury," he said with a grim smile. "I basically sat on the couch. It's a slow process to get the strength back to where it was. I slept in a chair for two months. I couldn't even do cardio. When I finally got back into it, I was dead after the first workout."

As spring progressed, however, Chris's body gradually readjusted. His workouts intensified, and by March, strength was returning.

He took solace watching his brother Rob compete in Super Bowl XLVI, held in his adopted town of Indianapolis. All the Gronkowski brothers and their father gathered there for the game. For a short time, Chris acted as host and tour guide. He also made appearances for the NFL's Play 60 program, which encourages children to be active for at least an hour per day.

"Every party that you go to offers free drinks," he recalled. "That week was pretty crazy. I did several charity events, so it was good to keep busy."

Entering his third NFL season in 2012, Chris was confident that he would be ready to perform in training camp. His challenge was to keep improving. In May 2012, he was traded to the Denver Broncos, a team with high expectations thanks to Peyton Manning's arrival as quarterback. On the business front, Chris was entering the final year of the first pro contract he signed. Three years; three teams. He anticipated that securing a roster spot in the fall would be a dogfight.

Chris expects to use his business training in some capacity — he has an accounting degree from Arizona — but is not sure what life will be like after the NFL. He wants to keep the door open to all possibilities, which is why he was excited to attend Harvard for a week with fellow football players.

"Once you stop going to school, you lose a little of your smarts," he said. "In the NFL, you can be cut anytime. I learned that in Dallas. I started pretty much my entire rookie year, and the next year I was gone. Playing football is a year-to-year situation."

Rob looks at the results of a photo shoot for *Muscle and Fitness* magazine, 2012. *Photo by Jeff Schober.*

Rob quickly became a Patriots fan favorite.

9

A New Generation of Tight Ends

"I'm proud of [Rob]. With his size and speed, already he's one of the most impressive athletes that has ever played that position."

— DREW ROSENHAUS

URING THE PAST SEVERAL years, the NFL has seen the tight end position evolve at a brisk pace. Traditionally, tight ends were linemen who blocked, clearing the way for a featured running back. Occasionally, the tight end would catch a pass after the quarterback progressed through options and found no open receivers, only the big man who dropped underneath the defense's coverage. The play was simply a check-down throw, a way to gain a few positive yards and keep the offense moving. Rarely was it the first choice for offensive production.

There were exceptions, of course. Mike Ditka and Kellen Winslow starred at the position in generations past.

But recently, NFL tight ends have become featured receivers. A new breed of super-athletes with size and speed has led to an offensive explosion at the position.

s are getting bigger and faster, and they're matchup nares," said Drew Rosenhaus, an agent whose firm represents many starting NFL tight ends. "Look at Rob Gronkowski. He's a freak. He can run a four-five forty. He's strong as an ox. He's nearly two hundred and seventy pounds. How do you tackle him? He's like a defensive end running with the football. He's a tank who runs like a deer."

While Rob is an elite tight end, he is not the only player at that position to shine. Statistics illustrate that the league is entering a golden age for tight ends, and the changes are happening quickly.

In 2011, seven tight ends finished the regular season with seventy-five catches or more. Only three years before, in 2008, there were four. And a decade earlier, in 2001, there were none. Tony Gonzalez of Kansas City and Shannon Sharpe of Baltimore tied for the league lead with seventy-three catches that year.

In 2011, seventeen tight ends had fifty or more catches, and another finished with forty-nine. In 2001, only six tight ends caught fifty or more balls.

More statistical evidence: Ditka, the Hall of Famer long considered the gold standard for tight ends, finished his twelve-year career with forty-three touchdown receptions. After only two seasons, Rob Gronkowski has accrued twenty-seven.

"The tight end position is taking off," San Francisco's Vernon Davis boasted to the Associated Press during the 2011 playoffs. "It's almost as if you have to start playing tight ends with cornerbacks nowadays because they're fast; these guys are strong and they're making plays like wide receivers."

Davis — who was a college teammate of Dan Gronkowski's

at the University of Maryland — is another freak tight end, with a mixture of size and speed. Besides Rob Gronkowski and his teammate Aaron Hernandez, the list of monster tight ends includes Jimmy Graham from New Orleans, Brandon Pettigrew from Detroit, Kellen Winslow II from Tampa Bay (the son of a Hall of Famer), and Jermichael Finley from Green Bay. Still in the mix is longtime star Tony Gonzalez, playing in Atlanta.

Jimmy Graham provides an interesting snapshot of a modern tight end. He arrived at football after being a high school hoops star and playing basketball for four seasons at the University of Miami. During his fifth year of college, he switched to the Hurricanes' football team, achieving enough success to be noticed at the sport. He was drafted by New Orleans in the third round in 2010.

Likewise, Rob Gronkowski was a high school basketball player. Although he enjoyed the sport and dominated on the court, he chose to pursue football professionally. His coach believes he could have earned a basketball scholarship and been a Division I player.

"I think kids who grew up on basketball courts are now realizing that they can play tight end and if they're good enough, they can make some money in the NFL," observed Dana Dimel, a longtime college football coach who is the offensive co-coordinator and running backs and tight ends coach at Kansas State University.

Dimel held the same position at the University of Arizona from 2006 to 2008 when Rob and Chris starred there. It was his innovation that put Chris on the field as an H-back to complement Rob at tight end.

"The high school basketball player can be a tremendous football player," Dimel said. "You want those soft hands, the ability to post people up, to use your body and get yourself open with your back turned to an opponent. Those are all skills a good tight end needs to have."

Chuck Swierski, Rob's high school basketball coach at Williamsville North, sees certain connections between basketball and football when he watches Rob excel in the NFL.

"A lot of his talent is God-given ability," Swierski noted. "But there was a play I watched where Robbie ran across the middle, stopped, and used his body to keep the defender at bay. Because of that, he was able to receive the ball. The commentator said that's like a post move in basketball. I don't know if I had anything to do with teaching him that one, but that's the connection between the two sports. Rebounding is just like getting position on a pass. It's using your body to shield off the defender. Now add a guy like Tom Brady who puts the ball wherever he wants. Robbie does his job by creating that space and Brady puts it there."

Bigger offensive players are more difficult to defend. Matchup problems immediately ensue for defenses. Should a defense double-team a star receiver? Fine, but that leaves the mega-tight-end in a one-on-one matchup with a smaller safety. By using size and position, the tight end is often able to create space and gain a completion.

Ozzie Newsome, a Hall of Fame tight end who played with the Cleveland Browns and is now the general manager of the Baltimore Ravens, reflected on the changing role of the position.

"When I was playing, the majority of tight ends w
of-attack guys," he told an Associated Press newspape.
"You would line up on the line of scrimmage next to the tackle
and were basically two-back oriented. Now, tight ends are getting opportunities to be extended away from the tackles, able
to stand up on the outside as receivers. These guys are getting
taller, bigger, and faster, or as fast as guys in the past. If you were
six three, two forty-five, you were a big tight end at that time,
and now they go six five, two sixty or two seventy and are just as
athletic."

Perhaps the word "revolution" overstates the emergence of
the tight end. If so, "evolution" seems too weak a word. No NFL
team better embodies the shift in tight-end productivity than
the New England Patriots.

In the 2010 NFL draft, Rob Gronkowski was selected in the
second round. Having left college early, even without playing
most of his junior year, Rob was expected to be a star, with his
unique mix of size, speed, and athleticism. Most teams would be
satisfied with acquiring such talent, considering a need had been
addressed at that position. With subsequent draft picks, the general manager would choose other areas in which to develop the
team.

But the Patriots do not always follow conventional wisdom.
How could it hurt to have another tight end in the lineup who
was a receiving threat as well? Coach Bill Belichick, after all,
once said that pass-catching tight ends who earn big money "are
direct descendants of Kellen Winslow."

In the fourth round of the same draft, 113th overall, the Patriots selected Aaron Hernandez, a highly regarded tight end from

the University of Florida. Although considered undersized at six one, 245 pounds, Hernandez was another outstanding tight end prospect, thanks to his speed and hand-eye coordination. How would New England integrate two rookies into a position that many NFL teams considered an afterthought?

"I really like what New England did with Rob," Dimel said. "Some people put a knock on him coming out that said he needed to work on his blocking, but I said that's one area he excels at. Rob can do everything, so they use him in different roles, and a guy like Hernandez, who's a little undersized, they use as a halfback or a route runner."

Statistics from 2010 illustrate that neither rookie took a back seat. The pair combined for eighty-eight receptions, more than 1,100 yards, and sixteen touchdowns. Hernandez had forty-five catches for 563 yards with six touchdowns; Gronkowski added forty-three receptions for 546 yards and ten touchdowns. Not only could two star tight ends exist together, they could both thrive in a potent offense.

Two star tight ends on one roster? It is a philosophical shift from just a few years earlier, when most pro teams did not even feature one.

Dan Gronkowski understands the seismic changes that are taking place at the tight end position. Having played with four NFL teams, including a role as the third tight end in New England's innovative offense, he has seen a variety of methods to employ the position to its maximum advantage.

"Tight ends used to be just for blocking," he said. "Now people are realizing in advanced offenses that you can get somebody on the field to confuse defenses. It's tough to get reads off a guy like Rob who's good at blocking and receiving. Then you throw another guy out there like Hernandez, who's a great receiving tight end, and defenses start thinking it's a passing situation, but you can surprise them with a run, because they're capable of that too. It's really about messing with a defense and putting different things out there so they have to react."

With tight ends becoming bigger, part of Dan's off-season goal was to add pounds and strength to his already large frame. He knows that getting a matchup advantage is always the goal, and he wants to help the Cleveland Browns achieve that. His brother already possesses size.

"Rob is bigger, stronger, and faster than any other tight end," Dan said. "When you put him against a safety, he can use his body against the defender. If you put him against a linebacker, he's going to be quicker than a linebacker. So no matter how you try to defend him, he's going to beat you."

Receiving is only part of the equation. In college, Dan was taught that if he wanted to get on the field, it was essential that he excel at blocking, effectively moving a defender off the line of scrimmage. It remains a basic requirement for a tight end.

"I used to teach Rob when he watched me in college," Dan said. "But now I'm taking pointers from him. His strength has taken over. Watch the film on Rob, and it's amazing. He's driving guys five yards off the ball. He's not only the best receiving tight end, he's also the best blocking tight end in the NFL. Part of the reason is that he works hard at that too."

"Short of Tom Brady, I think Rob Gronkowski is as dominating a player as there is on the Patriots," said Tony Massarotti, a talk show host and former reporter for the *Boston Herald* and *Boston Globe*. Massarotti has been writing and talking about sports in Boston for more than twenty years.

"It's early to say this, but I think he's the best tight end in the league and has a shot at being one of the great players in team history," Massarotti said. "He's the rarest of the rare. He's big, strong, fast, and has great hands. There's nothing he cannot do. If you look at great blocking tight ends in history, Gronkowski has to be in the conversation. If you look at catching the ball, he's right there too. Put it together and I'm not sure there's anyone quite like him."

Most pundits agree that part of an athlete's greatness is tied to longevity. It is far too early in Rob's career to put him in context, but there is little doubt that he has potential to erase many long-standing records.

"Health issues have affected him," Massarotti conceded. "But what he's done in his first few years is ridiculous. If he stays on this path, he'll go down as one of the greatest, if not the greatest."

Rosenhaus, agent for the three Gronkowski brothers, recited a list of tight ends he represents in the NFL. But he knows that Rob stands out.

"We have a lot of great tight-end clients, ranging from Kellen Winslow, Jeremy Shockey, Benjamin Watson, and Randy McMichael," he said. "We recruited Rob as the first- or second-ranked tight end going into his draft. I'm proud of him. With his size and speed, already he's one of the most impressive athletes that has ever played that position."

Rob as a one-year-old, 1990.

Sporting a tricorn hat and his Patriots jersey, Rob flashes a smile.

10

Rob: The Superstar

"I was always the one getting picked on and beat up, but it was a blast. We probably played for four hours every day. Three of the four were great, but at least one hour each day was spent fighting."

— ROB GRONKOWSKI

TEAMMATES ON THE NEW ENGLAND Patriots affectionately refer to him as Frankenstein. His body is often described as "freakish." As a kid, his Little League baseball coach called him "the Gorilla."

Rob Gronkowski is a physical specimen like almost no one else.

During their formative years, most of the Gronkowski boys hit a growth spurt during high school. Gordie took a little longer — he grew during his first year of college.

Not so for Rob. He was always bigger than boys his own age.

"The first time I met him, I was ten years old," said childhood friend John Ticco. "I was playing on a Little League baseball team, and this kid showed up. He was already six feet tall. I looked up at him and asked, 'Whose brother are you?'"

Rob stared back. "What do you mean about a brother? I'm on your team."

"You can't be on my team," Ticco replied. "You're too old."

When Rob insisted, Ticco used a ten-year-old's logic, pressing Rob to recite his birth date. The answer came back: May 14, 1989. Ticco's jaw dropped: he was actually two weeks older than this giant kid.

Years later, Ticco laughs at the story.

"I had never seen somebody that big before who was my age."

Another boyhood friend, Charlie Teal, remembers bragging to his father about Rob's athletic prowess, only to be met with doubt.

"In eighth grade, I told my dad I had a buddy who could dunk a basketball, and he didn't believe me," Teal said. "But it was true. We were playing driveway basketball, and Rob ran up, jumped over two kids, and dunked one-handed. He was so much bigger and stronger than everybody else."

It wasn't long before his skills were being noticed by high school coaches. As a freshman, Rob was elevated to the junior varsity basketball team, where he played for a few games before being bumped up to varsity. By his second game, he was entrenched as the starter.

"A freshman playing varsity? That never happens," said Chuck Swierski, Williamsville North's varsity basketball coach. "He was successful immediately. He didn't start that first game, but it was obvious that we needed him. With him playing center, we got to the sectional semifinals, and he was the reason why."

Swierski echoed the sentiments of Teal, almost word for word.

"In high school, Robbie was so much bigger, so much stronger, so much faster than everybody else. He had a man's body, but he was a kid. He was always giggling, always saying goofy stuff."

Rob is quick to credit his athletic success to growing up in a competitive household. He took cues from his three older brothers, working hard and finding an extra gear to match their abilities.

"My older brothers were bigger and better than me, so I always had to pick up my game because I was facing them all the time," Rob reflected. "I saw how they were trying to improve and what it took for me to get on their level, so I was always imitating them, doing what they were doing, but at a younger age. I got a competitive advantage there."

The Gronkowski home was a hotbed of athletic activity during their boyhood. Usually there was a game being played, whether it was basketball, pickup baseball, or football in the backyard. If it was too cold, or grew too dark, to play outside, it was off to the basement for a game of mini-stick hockey. Tiny sticks were the perfect size for young boys. As they aged, the kids continued playing—on their knees. Rob remembers these games fondly.

"Growing up in our house was pretty wild," he admitted with a wide smile. "Being the fourth-youngest, I wanted to play with my older brothers, because Goose was four years younger than me. So I was always the one getting picked on and beat up, but it was a blast. We probably played for four hours every day. Three of the four were great, but at least one hour each day was spent fighting."

Being a young brother meant Rob had to scratch and claw for any ounce of respect. Fights between Rob and Chris were frequent and particularly nasty. Recalling their battles, Chris explained the pecking order in the family.

"I beat up Rob every day," Chris said. "The kid had some problems but he never stopped, so we had to go to the next level. All the brothers used to go to the next brother up for a challenge. Dan went to Gord. I went to Dan. So Rob went to me, but sometimes he'd leapfrog to Dan. When we were kids, Dan was huge. He was always the biggest kid in the room. So you see? Rob was crazy."

The competitive spirit ran deep throughout the family, something noticed by friends and coaches over the years. Every brother wanted bragging rights over the next.

"I think their competitiveness came from the dinner table, to be honest," laughed Mike Mammoliti, the varsity football coach at Williamsville North High School. "You sit around with those five guys, and it's survival of the fittest. God bless their mom for being a good cook."

Gordy declared that Rob was never a shy boy. He was "a goofball," according to his father. Rob followed household rules, but occasionally needed a stern redirection to get back on track. He displayed a mischievous side and enjoyed pushing boundaries to see how much he could get away with.

"Rob is the class clown," Diane said. "He has to be goofing around."

"He took his mother to the limits all the time," Gordy said. "He used to get a kick out of that. He'd test you to see how far he could take you. If he knew he could get under your skin, you were in trouble."

Gordy cited two examples from Rob's childhood that show how he reveled in pushing people's buttons.

"One time he had on those stupid pants where his butt crack was showing and the waist hung down toward his knees. That pissed off his mother. She was in the kitchen with a big metal spoon and went whipping after him. Robbie took off running, but with the pants hanging down, the dummy fell flat on his face. She was hitting him in the ass with the spoon, and it was hysterical. I watched the whole thing and I couldn't stop laughing."

The other instance began during a family vacation. There is a themed restaurant in Myrtle Beach, South Carolina, that distributes paper hats to its customers, and people write silly slogans there. Diane's mother, the boys' grandmother, was given a hat that read "Grandma just cut the cheese." Silly. Not meant to be serious. But Rob took the joke and ran with it.

"Every time he'd see his grandma after that, he wouldn't let up on her," Gordy said. "She'd walk in a room and he'd groan and wave a hand in front of his face. He'd say, 'Pee-eww! Grandma, did you cut the cheese again?' He knew it bothered her, but he'd never let up."

• • •

Fostered by the competitive atmosphere at home, Rob desired to be better than anyone else on the field or court. As with his brothers, workouts began in eighth grade. By the time he entered high school, his size and developing body immediately caught the eyes of coaches. He played football, basketball, and baseball, finding success in all three.

"In high school, I liked basketball and football about the same," Rob noted. "But I knew I wanted to play football in college. That was where my area was. Basketball was fun, but in college, I would have been an undersized center. I felt I had the skills to bring it to the next level in football. That's where I could develop more."

Swierski, Rob's high school basketball coach, disputes Rob's belief that he would have struggled playing college hoops.

"I believe that if he wanted to, he could have been a Division One basketball player," Swierski said. "He only played for four months of the year. He never played organized basketball in the off-season. Once or twice I got him to come out, but he wouldn't touch a ball from the end of the season until he came back again the following November, and still he would absolutely dominate."

Swierski recalled his team playing an early-season game in Niagara Falls against a regional powerhouse from Syracuse. The gym was packed with spectators.

"The other team had a seven-foot center who had signed to play college ball at Michigan," he said. "Robbie caught a ball, turned on this kid, went up, and dunked. It was a one-step approach and he dunked with his opposite hand."

Many local high school coaches sat in the bleachers watching the matchup. They were there to see a great game but also to scout Williamsville North. When Rob dunked, Swierski happened to look across the gym floor.

"I looked at one coach who pulled out his inhaler and gave himself a quick shot. It was almost like he was thinking, 'How am I going to defend against this kid?' As a coach, if you're lucky you get the once-in-a-lifetime athlete. That was Robbie."

Rob played junior varsity football as an eighth and ninth grader. During his freshman year, he was called up to the varsity team for the playoffs, where he shared the field with his brother Chris, then a junior.

"We brought him up to the varsity team when he was a sophomore," Mammoliti said. "It was a no-brainer. He dominated from the get-go. Rob just had this fun streak about him. He loved playing. He loved being competitive."

During his years playing in Williamsville, Rob put up big numbers as a receiver and defensive end. But entering his senior season, in the fall of 2006, several events converged that caused Rob to leave Western New York to finish high school at Woodland Hills, outside Pittsburgh.

"There were a variety of reasons," Gordy said. "The biggest thing was that I was overseeing construction of a building in Pittsburgh. I had five stores in the area at the time. I lived in an apartment there so I could be part of everything. During his senior year, Rob wanted to live with me."

The broken basketball backboard at a rival school became an issue when people asked Rob to autograph pieces of it, on the expectation that he would soon become a professional sports star. Some adults wanted him prosecuted for the backboard incident. A separate allegation that he was involved in a fight outside school went unproven.

"All sorts of stuff were happening," Gordy explained. "People were gunning for Rob. It was stupid."

Once Rob's move became public, the issue went national when a reporter asked Gordy if he anticipated better-quality football in Pennsylvania.

"I told the reporter that Rob came to Pittsburgh with me because he wanted to spend his senior year making a choice about where to play college football, and it was convenient because I had a construction project going on there," Gordy said. "But the reporter didn't run with that part of the story. He ran with the part that Rob was coming down for better football. You can't transfer into a new high school to do that. That was the big controversy."

High school teams are not allowed to stack rosters with star players. Although that was not the intention, critics saw it differently. The debate raged: should a kid be allowed to transfer to a new high school if its sports are more competitive?

"We had to go to court," Gordy said. "National talk shows picked up the story. Some asked why a kid shouldn't be allowed to do this. But that wasn't the reason he moved, it's just that everyone knew that playing football was going to be Rob's profession. If a kid transfers to a great music or academic school, no one says anything about someone wanting to better himself in his chosen profession."

Still, comparisons were inevitable. Around Buffalo, Rob had played before a few hundred spectators at high school games.

Near Pittsburgh, crowds sometimes swelled to eight or ten thousand. It was a bigger stage, a bigger audience, higher expectations.

Years later, Rob is frank about playing at Woodland Hills.

"It's a whole different level in Pennsylvania," he admitted. "The quality of play was better. We had eight guys go to Division One schools that year, and a lot more going to Division Two and Three schools, as did the other teams we played. It was definitely good competition. When I first got there, I struggled."

Mammoliti, the football coach at Williamsville North, recalled Rob's difficult decision to leave.

"It was probably the worst phone call I've had," he said. "We talked it through. It was a shame, because, like anything else, you want the kid to finish with you and finish with his friends. I think part of him felt like he was letting us down. The reality is, there was no one else like him around. Hands down, he would have been All–Western New York. As a junior he caught fifty passes, and I could have thrown to him another twenty-five times, which I probably would have done as a senior."

Although he was upset to not work with Rob during his senior year, Bill Gorman, an assistant basketball coach at Williamsville North, remained in close contact even after Rob went to Pennsylvania.

"From a football standpoint, it was good that he went to Woodland Hills. He wasn't the focal point of the offense there. He had to learn how to block. At North, he didn't. Every play, they sent him out wide and expected him to catch a pass in front of four kids."

At Woodland Hills, Rob's receiving numbers dropped, but he

still garnered national attention. At season's end, he was named a SuperPrep All-American, PrepStar All-American, Associated Press Class 4A all-state, in addition to several regional awards from Pittsburgh-area newspapers.

In retrospect, Rob believes that transferring schools helped accelerate his development.

"If I had stayed at Williamsville North, I would have been used in a different role," he said. "I only had eight catches my whole year in Pittsburgh, where I probably would have had fifty or sixty in New York. But moving definitely helped me become a better blocker and a more complete player. I blocked on just about every play, and that helped going into my freshman year at college."

Thanks to his high profile, Rob was recruited far and wide, from virtually every big-name school. But he chose the University of Arizona early on. He had visited the school a few years earlier with Chris and their father when Chris was being recruited there. Arizona kept after Rob once Chris landed at Maryland.

"They were the first school to offer anything to me, and I already saw the campus and loved it there," Rob said. "The weather, the schooling, the coaching staff. I saw an opportunity for me to play right away. Those four things got me excited. I knew deep down that was the place to be."

Rob was the only brother who did not spend a year as a redshirt. He took the field immediately, playing as a true freshman. He credits the year spent in Pittsburgh with advancing his development.

"I consider my senior year of high school like my freshman

year, because when I got to college I wasn't homesick or anything," he noted. "I was ready to go. I knew what to expect going into a new program."

"In the middle of Rob's freshman year, Gordy and I went to Arizona for a visit," Gorman recalled. "I was talking to some of the assistant coaches when Gordy was wandering around. The coaches told me they knew Robbie was going to be special from the very first practice."

The story relayed to Gorman was that a star senior linebacker, later drafted into the NFL in the first round, had the reputation as a big man on campus. At the first team workout, the quarterback tossed the ball to Rob on a seven-yard out pattern, and this linebacker came across the field with fire in his eyes, leveling Rob. He then stood over him.

"Welcome to the real world, high school All-American," the senior taunted. "That doesn't mean shit here."

Rob got up, undaunted. A few plays later, he caught the same pass and dashed up the field. The same linebacker was running toward him. Players are coached to step out of bounds to avoid unnecessary contact. Instead, Rob cut toward him, lowered his shoulder, and blasted the defender, running him over. He then shed another linebacker's block. It took a third player to finally trip him up.

"The whole offense was going crazy," Gorman recounted. "Robbie stood up, went over to the linebacker lying on the ground, and dropped the ball onto his chest. Nobody ever challenged Rob like that again."

• • •

At college, Rob continued to grow as a player. In 2007, he recorded twenty-eight catches for 525 yards with six touchdowns. He led the team in yards-per-reception average, at 18.8. The awards rolled in: *The Sporting News* Freshman All-American, Rivals.com Freshman All-American, *The Sporting News* freshman Pac-10, and All-Pac-10 honorable mention.

Despite missing the first three games of his sophomore campaign, Rob recorded forty-seven catches for 672 yards and ten touchdowns. Twice he was named the John Mackey Tight End of the Week, an award given nationally. After setting school records for a tight end in single-game, single-season, and career receptions, yards, and touchdowns, Rob was named an Associated Press third-team All-American and All-Pac-10 first-team tight end.

Everything was going right. It didn't take a crystal ball to project that Rob was likely to shine in the NFL. With two years of college eligibility, already he was being projected as a first-round draft pick.

During the off-season after his sophomore year, however, Rob injured his back, underwent surgery, and sat out an entire season.

"You have so much more respect for the game once you miss a whole season," he reflected. "You sit on the couch because that's basically all you can do, and you see your teammates out there, your brother. It's no fun watching them play. You want to be out there."

He ruminated about surgery, finally deciding that was the best way to proceed. During an extensive rehabilitation program, Rob worked to regain his old form. By strengthening his back and core, he helped minimize setbacks and flare-ups. Once healthy, he faced a major decision: should he return to play college football at Arizona or make the leap to the NFL, where his brother Dan was playing, and Chris, set to graduate, had a shot at making a team too?

"It was definitely a tough decision," he said. "But it was always a dream to play in the NFL. That was my goal ever since I knew I had a chance. I wanted to get there as soon as possible. Dan was already in the NFL, and Chris was going that year, so I thought we could help each other out. All three of us could be in the league at once, and you don't know how long that could last."

Rob considered the options and discussed the implications with his family. He considered all angles before deciding to turn pro.

"I loved the school," Rob confessed. "I wanted to come back and give Arizona another year because of everything they did for me. But sometimes you've got to do what's best for you. I wanted to get on the highest stage and go against the best competitors to bring out the best in me."

Yet there was a lingering obstacle: Rob was not fully healed in time to participate in the NFL combine, held for several days at the end of February into early March. Without an opportunity to work out before pro scouts, his draft status would remain uncertain. But he found a way around that: once Rob recovered, he hosted an exclusive pro day at Arizona. Scouts were invited to see him work out individually, joined by his brother Chris. A former college quarterback who lived in Tucson showed up to throw passes to the brothers.

"When we went out there, it was just me and Rob and another

kid," Chris recalled of the private tryout. The quarterback had played collegiately in Hawaii, graduating the year before. The brothers had never met him.

"It worked out real well even though we never had a chance to practice together before that day," Chris said. "Usually it's harder on the quarterback to throw to guys he's not familiar with, but he was pretty good. His passes were right on."

On a sunny spring day, some twenty-five scouts gathered at Arizona Stadium. Rob was the draw, but thanks to his family connections, Chris was in the spotlight as well.

"It was very cool," Chris said. "We walked onto the field without shirts, just to show off. We killed it that day. We caught every pass and ran so hard we were about to throw up. We really got after it. Rob had on blocking pads and I ran at him at full speed, then we switched. I was trying to drill him as hard as I could. I was so into it that my hand slipped a couple times, and I popped myself in the face. By the time it ended, my face was scratched from swatting the pads. It was like a badge of honor."

Any concerns about Rob's recovery had been answered. Now it was simply a question of anticipating the 2010 draft. The two highest-ranked tight ends were Rob and Jermaine Gresham.

"The draft was going to be about those two," Gordy said. "At least one was going to go in the first round, and we hoped both. We figured that the Cincinnati Bengals were taking a tight end with the twenty-first pick, but we didn't know which. Gresham had played at Oklahoma, so we thought Cincy would take him because some of the coaches there were from Oklahoma."

Once that happened, the Gronkowskis reasoned that Rob would be the next tight end off the board. Baltimore, drafting twenty-fifth, had expressed interest in adding a tight end. But the Ravens traded their pick to Denver, who quickly selected quarterback Tim Tebow.

"When the trade happened, we looked at the rest of the picks," Gordy said. "We thought maybe Kansas City would take him—or the Bills. But neither happened. When it came into the second round, New England knew that Baltimore was going to take Rob, so the Patriots traded up to get him ahead of the Ravens."

Rob was drafted in the second round, forty-second overall. He recalled the various emotions that came with waiting to be selected.

"Emotions were flying high," he said. "You want to get drafted in the first round. That was my goal, but it didn't work out that way. Looking back, I kind of had a feeling I wasn't going to go in the first round."

His limited college experience put him at a disadvantage. Rob played as a freshman and sophomore—although he missed three games that season—then sat out his entire junior year at Arizona. He had only appeared in twenty college games, compared to seniors who had logged forty-eight over a four-year span.

"Plus I was young," he added. "I didn't participate in my combine at all. I only did one little pro day. That's all the scouts had to base me on. I wanted to go in the first round, but it would have been a long shot."

Any disappointment of dropping into the second round evaporated quickly. The Patriots had piled up Super Bowl rings in the previous decade. With Rob on their roster, why couldn't they add to the collection?

"Once I was drafted, it was a great emotional feeling," Rob

else disappeared. I was still chosen pretty high, ⌐ a great situation. You couldn't ask for anything ⌐w England had a great quarterback and head coach. ⌐nking about it now, if you get drafted into the right situation, it doesn't matter whether you drop down in the draft. The ranking doesn't mean anything. It's what you do from there on out."

For a twenty-one-year-old rookie, entering training camp in Foxborough might have been intimidating. In one corner of the locker room was superstar quarterback Tom Brady. Nearby was receiver Randy Moss. Head coach Bill Belichick, patrolling the halls with a perpetual scowl, was widely considered a football mastermind. Yet Rob was undaunted by the talent surrounding him. He just wanted to play.

"One thing about Rob: he's never been enamored of superstars," Gorman said.

Rob was determined to make an impact. He immediately won the admiration of Patriots' fans in a preseason game against St. Louis. Catching a pass at the five-yard line, he was corralled around the ankles by a defender. But he did not go down. Maintaining balance, he drove his massive legs toward the goal line and plunged forward. Referees initially called him down at the one-yard line, but a coach's challenge reversed the call to a touchdown.

The play lasted mere seconds, but it provided a snapshot of Rob's determination. Afterward, radio announcers declared, "We need to start calling him Gronk."

Video of the play is on YouTube, titled "The Moment When Rob Gronkowski Became Gronk."

He continued to impress in preseason, scoring four touchdowns. In his first regular-season game against Cincinnati, he snagged a one-yard pass from Brady in the fourth quarter. In week ten, he caught three touchdowns against Pittsburgh, the youngest rookie in NFL history to achieve that. During a December game against the Bills in his hometown of Buffalo, he caught two more, then finished the year with one more touchdown the following week. For the regular season, he accumulated ten.

He was the first rookie tight end since the NFL–AFL merger in 1970 to score ten touchdowns. Rob did not miss a game or practice all season, starting eleven of the sixteen games. On the year, he caught forty-two passes for 546 yards.

By all accounts, it was a successful start to his NFL career. What would year two bring?

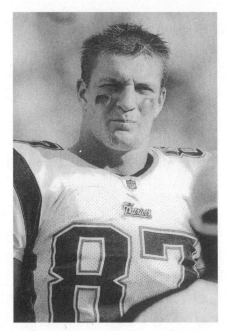

Rob, focused for game day in the NFL.

Patriots fans show their appreciation for Gronk.

11

Rob Explodes

"Being in the media is pretty crazy. I'm just being myself. I've been the same guy for the last ten years, but suddenly whatever I do is in the media."

— ROB GRONKOWSKI

I T WAS AUGUST 2011, a few weeks before the NFL season's kickoff. Sitting behind his desk at G&G Fitness, Gordy Gronkowski leaned back, locking hands behind his thick neck. His son Rob was coming off a rookie season in which he posted impressive numbers and improved with each game. By year's end, he had caught ten touchdowns and become an offensive force.

"Robbie is going to catch fifteen TDs this year," Gordy predicted.

Such boldness was difficult to take seriously. This was a proud father, after all, boasting about his son. The touchdown record for tight ends was thirteen, set by Antonio Gates in 2004, then equaled by Vernon Davis in 2009. True, the New England Patriots was an upper-echelon team with a great quarterback, but could a second-year player — still more about promise than performance — really challenge those statistics?

Turns out Gordy underestimated his boy's output. Rob caught seventeen touchdown passes, rushed for another, and added three more in the playoffs.

A few weeks after the Super Bowl, when reminded of the healthy skepticism surrounding that summer prediction, Gordy didn't miss a beat.

"Why does everybody doubt me?" he said with a grin.

"Entering 2011, I felt I had a good rookie season the year before," Rob reflected. "I really appreciated the support of my teammates and coaches. The rookie year is so hard, learning the playbook and system. Your mind is hectic at all times. Going into the second year, I was more settled. I knew the playbook, knew what was expected of me, how everything is run. I was way more comfortable. Obviously, I wanted to progress from the first year and help the team more."

Mission accomplished. The 2011 season will be remembered as the year Rob exploded in the NFL. His performance on the field was matched only by the attention — sometimes controversial — that he drew off it.

During interviews, Rob pauses after hearing a question, then answers quickly, speaking in fast chunks. Despite his intelligence, answers sometimes settle into clichés.

"I just want to keep grinding and work hard."

Or, "I'll do whatever it takes to help the team."

Part of this is the burden of a high-profile athlete. Rob is accustomed to being asked questions, more often than many of his teammates. ESPN, the *Boston Globe,* and *Sports Illustrated* are always hunting for a quote. Everyone wants a piece of his time. Strangers who recognize him approach and ask for money. A letter from a high school sophomore in Boston includes a cell number, asking Rob to please phone the kid's girlfriend and wish her a happy birthday because it would make her day.

"We've talked about how he needs to be careful," said former coach Bill Gorman. "I tell him, the only people you owe anything to are your mother and father. That's it."

Who wouldn't be wary of it all? Rob cares less for words and more about on-field performance. Why, he wonders, can't that be a primary means of communication?

"Being in the media is pretty crazy," Rob reflected. "I'm just being myself. I've been the same guy for the last ten years, but suddenly whatever I do is in the media. It's weird, because I've kind of had to change my lifestyle. I've got to watch what I say and do, because little things can get out and blow up and become national news. I have to be careful where I am and what I say. At first it's hard, but I've seen what's going on and tried to adjust to it."

Through it all, Rob maintains the hint of a grin, a perpetual smile. Life is fun and, despite the attention, he wants to enjoy it.

"There is a time to be serious and a time to not be serious, and you have to know when that is," Rob reflected. "When it's practice time and lifting time, you're grinding, going full speed, working hard. You can goof around when you're playing with your buddies. But come game time, it's all business. I'm serious and ready to go."

Some of his longtime friends have witnessed Rob's commitment firsthand over the years.

"In high school and college, he took the off-the-field requirements way more seriously than everyone else," said Charlie Teal, the high school classmate of Rob's who also attended the University of Arizona. "In the summer, Rob got up early to swim, worked out real quick, then took a nap, and worked out with all of us later that day."

"He's worked extremely hard to get where he is," added John Ticco, another high school friend. "Not a lot of people understand that. I've heard people say, 'If I was six six and two sixty-five, I could be in the NFL too.' They don't understand Rob's discipline. He knows when to be serious. There are guys that are bigger than him, but their minds aren't right for it and they flame out."

In 2011, Rob had the best statistical year of any tight end in NFL history. His ninety catches were second to Jimmy Graham's ninety-nine, but Rob led tight ends with 1,327 yards and eighteen touchdowns. Twenty-two of his receptions went more than twenty yards, and sixty-nine of them were for first downs. He had zero fumbles.

In only his second year, Rob evolved into a complete player. He could block, run, and catch with acumen. Having a quarterback with pinpoint accuracy made him even more valuable. But the level of success surprised Rob himself.

"I felt I could improve on my rookie year and have a solid second season," he said six weeks after the Super Bowl. "But I mean, I wasn't expecting anything like that. It took off to another level. I had catches every game and scored a few touchdowns. The reason was because everyone was working together. Having a great support cast around me was one of the keys."

When the Patriots entered the 2011 playoffs after winning the AFC East, it appeared there was little that could slow the team's momentum. Quarterback Tom Brady, receiver Wes Welker, and tight ends Gronkowski and Aaron Hernandez combined to form a potent offense. In the first two playoff games, Rob had fifteen receptions and three touchdowns. All was going according to plan.

Then, during a tackle by Baltimore safety Bernard Pollard in the AFC Championship game, Rob's left ankle rolled awkwardly. He refused to stay down, leaping up toward the huddle with a pronounced limp. He sat out but returned a few plays later, insistent on ignoring the pain.

"Medical professionals examined it after the game and told us the damage was done. It couldn't be hurt anymore," Gordy said. "We knew it was serious and that he needed surgery. He was going day to day. The tendons were stretched out. His agent and I were worried that he might favor it and hurt something else. If it wasn't the Super Bowl, he would have never been playing. But Rob is a tough kid and he wasn't going to be denied."

That sort of talk is irrelevant, Rob suggested.

"There was no point of thinking what to do if it was a normal week," he said. "It wasn't. It was Super Bowl week. Possibly

I'd have had surgery a couple days after the Baltimore game, but I can't really say. There was one more game to play, so we kept it going."

With no real controversies to feed off, the media played up Gronkowski's injury in the days leading up to the game.

"There was no other story to report on besides Rob's ankle," his father said. "Nobody on either team did anything stupid. No one broke curfew. There were no sightings of someone doing something dumb in a bar. So they ended up focusing on this ankle. It got more attention than it should have."

Unwillingly, Gordy found himself in the center of a media firestorm when he told a Buffalo TV station that his son would play in the Super Bowl despite the high-ankle sprain. At the time, the Patriots had not released information about the injury. Coach Bill Belichick is notorious for keeping such things confidential.

Fellow players found the incident comical.

"That's what his dad said?" New England receiver Deion Branch asked, giggling when he learned of the comments. "When did he say that? For real? That's good. I guess he knows. I don't know. I don't know what Gronk has."

"My comment went viral," Gordy said a few days later. "It changed everyone's perception of the outcome. When I got to Indianapolis, people stopped me and asked to take a picture with Papa Gronk. I waved at the cameras and zipped my lip. I didn't want to be part of the circus, but suddenly, I was."

Every question Rob faced was about his injury. Ever the prankster, Rob was not above having fun with it. "What are you asking *me* for?" he wondered. "Talk to my dad." With cameras rolling, he exaggerated a limp as he walked into one interview. When he finally did turn serious, the mantra he repeated was "Day to day."

In fact, Gordy's prediction was correct. Rob did compete in the Super Bowl, catching two passes for twenty-six yards. The New York Giants defeated the Patriots, 21–17.

Rob refused any suggestions that he was less than healthy during the game.

"I didn't get to practice for two weeks, and that's a big difference," he conceded. "But so what? I was out there, and there are no excuses. You have to give one hundred percent when you're on the field."

He was nearly a hero on the last play, a desperate Hail Mary throw toward the end zone. Despite being tipped, battered, and knocked about, the ball fell helplessly to the ground a few yards from Gronkowski's outstretched arms.

"You can't control where the Hail Mary is going," he said. "If the ball had bounced to the right, everyone would have said I was in the best spot. But it bounced to the left more and I just wasn't there. Obviously, since then I've wondered why I didn't keep running. I stopped and hoped the ball would bounce to my side. With a Hail Mary, it's all luck. It's painful to think about it."

"He could have been a legend if he'd caught that pass at the end," his father reflected. "If he had another step, he would have had it. A few days after the game, a TV program did an analysis that showed he was taking shorter steps because of his injury.

If it wasn't for his bad ankle, he would have been there to make that catch. But the big picture is that if it wasn't for his ankle, he would have caught eight or ten passes instead of two. There may have been a totally different outcome to the game."

Five weeks later, with his left ankle protected by a blue-and-white cast, Rob conceded that he had still not watched video of the play.

"I don't even want to see it," he said with resolve. "I just want the season to start so we get another shot."

During the 2011 season, as Rob's stature grew, he found himself in the spotlight for reasons besides football. In October, he returned to Arizona during the Patriots' bye week. During that visit, a mutual friend introduced him to a porn star, who posted photos of herself online wearing Rob's No. 87 Patriots jersey. He stood behind her, shirtless, both of them smiling.

Was this outrageous and embarrassing behavior or simply a twenty-two-year-old taking a photo with an attractive girl? Was it, as some claimed, the act of a young athlete trying to increase the number of followers on his Twitter account?

"I didn't intend anything to hurt the reputation of anyone on the New England Patriots or on behalf of [team owner] Robert Kraft," a contrite Rob said when the cameras gathered to question him after he returned to work the following week, preparing for an AFC matchup against Pittsburgh. "That's all, just a simple picture, that's all. From here on out, I'm just here to talk about the Pittsburgh Steelers and the big game this weekend."

More media attention followed, however, at a post–Super Bowl party, when video was released of a shirtless Rob dancing on a stage just a few hours after the loss.

"Once the game ended, there was a private party for Patriots fans," Rob's father said. Gordy attended with his other sons. "There were about a thousand people there. I think you had to win a lottery to get tickets. Earth, Wind and Fire kicked off the show, then Maroon Five, then LMFAO. That's when the craziness started."

According to Gordy, Patriots offensive lineman Matt Light jumped onstage and began dancing. Soon Rob followed suit.

"It was two in the morning and everyone was having a good time," Gordy said. "It was a good season. They had twenty-five really good weeks. Let's be honest: Robbie had some pretty good dance moves."

Critics complained because the Patriots had just lost the biggest football game of the year. Should team members really be out partying a few hours later?

Gordy, however, defended his son by focusing on the big picture. All five Gronkowski boys spent the week before kickoff in Indianapolis. They made several public appearances and were given the red carpet treatment. The boys turned up on TV shows, visited hospitals and army bases, and promoted the NFL's campaign to keep kids active. Despite the loss, a busy week had come to a close.

"The thing about Rob is, he's not the kind of guy to sit there and dwell," his father explained. "He was definitely very upset, no doubt about it, but after a time, he's onto the next thing. That's how he is. That's his personality. With all his brothers there, Rob wasn't going to dwell. Except for the result of the game, it had been a great week."

Months afterward, Rob remained upset about losing the biggest game of his career.

"I'm still not over it," he said. "It makes me want to keep working. You don't get the taste out of your mouth until the next season starts all over again and you get the first win under your belt."

The post–Super Bowl hoopla occurred late Sunday night, into the wee hours of Monday morning. As analysts dissected the matchup and bantered about the Patriots' postgame party over the next few days, Gordy returned home to Buffalo. But later that week, he was back in Boston to accompany Rob to his ankle surgery, scheduled for Friday morning.

Thursday night, however, Rob and his father attended a Celtics game at TD Garden. With courtside seating, Rob participated in a community-service event, sitting with a cancer patient for part of the game.

Walking into the arena, Gordy felt apprehension. His son had been popular in Boston for most of the past two years, but the Patriots just lost the Super Bowl and Rob had been filmed acting wild at a postgame party. Would fans understand and sympathize, or would they hold a grudge and turn on him?

"I wondered how people were going to react," Gordy admitted. "Were people pissed off because he had his shirt off a few nights earlier?"

When Rob stepped onto the floor, he towered over the people around him. A thrill rippled through the crowd. Thousands of people began clapping. Suddenly everyone was on their feet, yelling his nickname. The chant was deafening, echoing to the rafters. "Gronk! Gronk! Gronk!"

"Rob put his two arms on my shoulders and pushed me through," Gordy said. "It was like we were in a *Rocky* movie. I never would have expected that reaction in a million years. It was amazing. People went nuts for him. I was standing there thinking, holy shit, this is my son! It was one of the greatest moments I've had in my entire life."

Gordy's wonder did not stop that night. In the middle of the first quarter, Kobe Bryant of the Los Angeles Lakers ran past Rob.

"Hey, Gronk, I want to talk to you later," he said, glancing briefly at the football star, then continuing to trot up the court.

Gordy rubbed his eyes. Had that just happened? Did one of the biggest basketball stars on the planet request time with his son?

"After the game, Kobe came over and said, 'I've got to get my picture with you,'" Gordy recounted. "He said, 'Gronk, you've got to play for the Philadelphia Eagles because that's my favorite team.' So Kobe started recruiting him for the Eagles. The next day that was in the paper. Rob can't make a move without it being news. It's the craziest thing you've ever seen."

Interest in his personality had gone international. That week, Rob Gronkowski was the seventh-most-popular Internet search in the world.

"I need to get him out of the spotlight," his father lamented. "I've got to get the kid some rest."

There was little rest in the off-season. On a sunny spring Saturday in 2012, Dan, Chris, Rob, and their father gathered at Williamsville North High School, in the boys' old high school gym, to begin a daylong media marathon. *Muscle & Fitness* magazine was in town to capture images for a cover shot, scheduled to appear that fall. Photographers set up light stands before a gray backdrop that curled onto the floor. Amid power cords and an open laptop, equipment tested brightness and light quality. A folding makeup table, holding various hues and brushes, became a command post near the bleachers. Hovering nearby was the magazine journalist who had interviewed the brothers a day earlier.

As the Gronkowskis shook hands with the crew, Rob was immediately whisked to wardrobe. After removing his shirt and donning football pants, he stood as a makeup artist sprayed coloring onto his chiseled frame. While everyone else settled in, Rob was sent before the cameras.

Gordy moved about the gym like a salesman, shaking hands and speaking to everyone. Dan and Chris greeted their old high school coach, Mike Mammoliti, and said hi to the photographers and producers. While Rob was being photographed, they dribbled basketballs, practiced jukes, and launched three-pointers. Dan and Chris had been invited to participate for the day, but it was clear Rob was the featured player.

Standing near the backdrop, Rob appeared bored, requesting that music be played. Once he stepped onto the tarp, however, photographers began directing him, suggesting expressions. His movements became animated. The process stretched on and on.

"Rob, you suck as a model," Chris taunted ninety minutes later. "They still don't have a good shot yet!"

"Really glad we got up early for this," Dan commented, his words tinged with sarcasm. "But I shouldn't say that. I understand Rob is the draw. If it wasn't for Rob, we wouldn't even be invited today."

Finally, Dan, Chris, and even Gordy joined Rob as models, although their time in the spotlight lasted only fifteen minutes. The boys all removed their shirts; Gordy kept his white T-shirt on.

Meanwhile, ESPN's Jeremy Schaap arrived to spend the afternoon with the Gronkowski family in anticipation of an *E:60* segment about Rob to air in September, right around the time the New England Patriots would appear on *Monday Night Football*. Schaap entered the gym before lunchtime.

Once the photo shoot ended, the boys changed back into their street clothes and ESPN's cameramen snapped into action. Boom mikes stretched overhead as the four Gronkowskis huddled in a circle with Schaap, who questioned them about their younger days playing in the Williamsville North gym. This was followed by a trip to the weight room, where Chris pointed to a wallboard, boasting that he still held school records for lifting despite graduating seven years earlier.

After a quick trip to the football field, cameras and microphones chronicling every step, the entire crew agreed to meet at a nearby restaurant, where a buffet of pizza, subs, and chicken wings was spread on a common table. Under the patio's awning, several of the boys' friends gathered as well. With his back to the wall, Rob acted silly.

"When we were in high school, this kid was stopped by the cops," Rob said, pointing to his friend. "He crapped his pants."

Schaap and the ESPN camera crew took it all in.

Nearby patrons recognized Rob. A young boy approached timidly, requesting an autograph, to which Rob obliged.

After lunch, it was back to the Gronkowski family home, where their kitchen became a makeshift television studio. Tables and chairs were pushed aside, darkening film laid across the windows to reduce glare, and lights and cords snaked against the tile floor. Before Schaap began interviewing Rob, everyone aside from the crew was sent outside.

Next to the Gronkowskis' wide driveway is a tennis court with basketball posts and hockey nets pushed against the fence. Two dozen people, all banished from the house, lined up to shoot three-pointers in a family competition known as twenty-one. Gordy, Dan, Chris, and Gordie all launched basketballs toward the net. Goose, feeling under the weather, watched from an upstairs window, but shortly came down and joined as well.

Nearly an hour and a half later, with the third game underway, Gordie began to wonder what was taking so long.

"They're still in there interviewing Rob? Seriously? The kid only ever says two things." In his best Rob impression, he grunted, "I just want to keep grinding and working hard. Do what's best for the team." He shook his head. "Can't get two hours out of that."

· · ·

In the resulting *E:60* interview, Schaap referred to Rob as "the most irrepressible adolescent on the planet . . . uninhibited; juvenile."

Rob embraced the description. "I inspire people to act like children," he admitted.

Just ask his brothers, he said. When he was growing up, his plan was always to play in the NFL and do silly things. He was living his dream.

In the summer of 2012, Rob was seemingly everywhere. He appeared on the cover of *ESPN The Magazine*'s "body issue," in which athletes are photographed naked. Rob used an oversized confetti football to cover his private parts, but otherwise showed little inhibition. He and his brothers mugged on the red carpet at the ESPY Awards in California. Rob, Chris, and Dan appeared on *Young Hollywood,* a TV magazine show. Rob turned up in so many places that season, the media started referring to it as the Summer of Gronk.

"I don't really like that phrase," Rob admitted. "The summer was cool, but I was basically doing what I do every year. The highlight is being together with my family."

There was a reason for all the attention. Rob's play on the field created legitimate media and fan interest. In every game he played, he had the potential to dominate defenses, not simply by catching passes, but also by his fierce blocking on run plays. He had quickly grown into one of the NFL's biggest stars.

Football, Rob understands, has led to publicity. But he insists he would not act any differently if he had never played the sport.

"Really, I'm the same person I've been since high school. If I wasn't playing football, I'd be in the fitness industry. I'd love to train people or sell equipment, like what my dad does. My dad always taught us how to get to the next level. He brought us into the weight room and motivated us, put us into programs to develop our speed and agility. I could never be an accountant. If it wasn't football, I'd have to be active, running around, helping people out."

With so many demands on his time, Rob is selective about appearances. He contributes time to charitable events, but needs to strike a balance.

"I just lay everything out on the table," he said. "I try to figure out what the cause is for and how it fits with my practice and workout schedule. On the off-season, I work out about two hours each day. After that, if I can get to an event, I'll do it."

Despite having two years left on his first pro contract, Rob inked a six-year extension with the Patriots, making him the highest-paid tight end in league history. It seemed he couldn't get more popular. Despite having just turned twenty-three, he was all grown up. The Age of Gronk had arrived.

Goose, Gordie, and Rob opening presents on Christmas morning, 2003.

Goose as a high school football star, 2009.

12

Goose: Greatness Expected

"The one who beat me up most was Rob. But I figured
out a secret move I called the Treatment."

— GLENN "GOOSE" GRONKOWSKI

IN ADDITION TO BEGINNING a workout program upon
reaching eighth grade, one of the rites of passage for a Gronkowski boy was to be dubbed with a slang name by his father.

"When they were young, I had nicknames for all my boys,"
Gordy reflected. "Gordie was G-money. When I coached him
in baseball, any time the team needed a hit, he came through.
Danny looked like a monkey because his face was round, so I
called him Monkey Man. When he was younger, Chris was always getting into stuff, so I called him Critter Chris. Then when
he started playing hockey, we called him Chrissy Fontaine, after the Sabres' star Pat LaFontaine. Rob was always a slob, with
pants hanging down, so instead of Robbie, he was Slobbie."

None of those names stuck. But the youngest Gronkowski

brother, Glenn, is rarely referred to by his given name. Everyone simply addresses him as Goose.

"I have no idea how Goose got his nickname," Gordy admitted.

Ask Goose where he acquired the handle and his wide shoulders shrug, face lilting into a half grin.

"No one knows," he said simply, emanating boredom in response to a question he has fielded too many times.

All agree that Glenn was named for Gordy's older brother, a point of pride for the elder Glenn.

"They ran out of names, to be honest with you," he chuckled. "They named the boys after other people we knew, and my name was left over. From what people are saying, Goose is the fastest of all of them. A few years ago in a high school game, he caught an eighty-yard flea-flicker play. He seemed pretty fast then. Right now everyone expects good things from him."

Goose, born in 1993, is ten years younger than Gordie. At eighteen, he already stood six feet three inches and weighed 225. As he walked through his kitchen in sweatpants and a Buffalo Sabres T-shirt revealing burgeoning arms, his growing body showed evidence of weight training. But his frame is more developed than his facial features, which remained innocent, curious.

While the other boys are each two years apart, Goose is four years removed from Rob. When the eldest trained together with Demeris Johnson, Goose was too young to join, waiting until later to complete the program. Having watched his older brothers put in the hard work required for success, Goose witnessed firsthand the time and commitment it takes.

"Growing up, no one forced any of us into playing sports," Goose said. "I chose to do this, and I want to succeed and get to where my brothers are. With me following in their steps, I think it's easier. They've been there before so I can ask their advice. When I'm having a bad day and don't want to do this anymore, I think about how my brothers went through the same thing, and look at them now. It's a way for me to push myself."

His skills were sharpened by competing against his older siblings.

"The boys didn't care that he was younger," their mother recalled. "They threw him around. They figured, you want to play with us? OK, but you have to keep up. Glenn could do more because of his brothers."

In high school, Goose excelled in football, baseball, and in the classroom. After graduating in 2011 from Williamsville North, he was offered a scholarship to play H-back at Kansas State, where he began attending classes in January 2012.

Fall 2011 was a transitional time for the Gronkowskis. Gordie finished his baseball career, visited Western New York briefly, then moved to Cincinnati to help with the family business. Rob starred for the New England Patriots, racking up impressive numbers, and was joined by brother Dan, who started, then was cut and re-signed, cut again, and finally caught on with the Cleveland Browns. Chris, a fullback in Dallas the season before, found himself playing in Indianapolis, where the Colts struggled without quarterback Peyton Manning, winless in their first eight games. Chris's season ended with a torn pectoral muscle. Only Goose remained at home, taking a part-time job stocking shelves at a grocery store until he left for college in January. Despite the fact that his boys were spread across the country, Gordy remained connected to them.

"It doesn't seem like the boys are gone yet, because I travel to their games just about every weekend," Gordy said. "Goose goes with me most of the time. But I think it's going to be a reality check when he leaves for college in January and there's no football and the rest of the guys aren't in their hometown. Right now, he's like my best friend. It's going to be a rude awakening for me."

Being the youngest has its advantages. With his older brothers gone, Goose was able to experience life as the only child living at home.

With the absence of his brothers, Goose spent quality time with his father. They watched Kansas State football games or blocked out an evening for their favorite TV show, *Law and Order*. They often went skiing and snowmobiling together.

"If I'm not home, we talk every day on the phone," Gordy said. "He'll call and say, did you watch this show? Did you see that highlight from the game?"

The weekend he left for Kansas State in January, Gordy had a head cold that kept his voice hoarse. Dan, talking to his father on the phone, thought perhaps Gordy was choked up.

"You sure it's just a cold?" Dan teased.

During the spring of his senior year in high school, Goose focused on baseball, visiting two pro camps to measure his skills. In Ithaca, New York, he auditioned for the Los Angeles Dodgers, then traveled to Rochester to work out for the Minnesota Twins.

"They tested my hitting, arm strength, and speed," Goose

said. "The coaches run you through a quick batting practice, then have you do a sixty-yard dash, which is the distance between home and second base."

He hoped to be drafted out of high school, wanting to give that sport a try before committing to football. But his name was never called.

"If I had gotten drafted for baseball, I would have gone and played somewhere for three or four months because I wasn't going to be doing anything anyway," Goose said. "If I did well, I was going to stick with that, maybe. I wanted to keep my options open. I thought I did sweet at those tryouts."

Baseball teams may have been interested in Goose, but his full-ride scholarship for football at Kansas State probably worked against him. His upcoming gridiron career made teams reluctant to invest a draft pick, because odds were good that he would never play for them.

"I think I may have scared them away," Gordy admitted. "He was going to school anyway, so I told teams not to waste our time unless they came in with a contract offer over four hundred thousand. They couldn't give us peanut money. Once Goose didn't get drafted, he lost interest in that and just decided to concentrate on football."

Despite the influence of his oldest brother, football is in Goose's blood. As the baby of the Gronkowski family, for years he trolled the sidelines of varsity football games, watching players, observing rituals of the sport, and dreaming that one day he would grow up and compete like his brothers. As an eight- and nine-year-old, he served as ball boy for the Williamsville North varsity team.

"Everybody loved playing around with him," his father reflected. "Everybody knew who Goose was even when he was a little kid."

Mike Mammoliti, the football coach at Williamsville North, remembered his first encounter with the youngest Gronkowski brother.

"He was the ball boy when Dan was playing," Mammoliti said. "We had just kicked off in a night game, and all of a sudden I see this little kid sprint past me onto the field and grab the tee."

Mammoliti turned to one of his assistants. "Who is that?" he asked.

"That's the Goose."

"Who's the Goose?" Mammoliti wondered. "I called him Glenn up until then. But as he got older, he developed in his own way."

As in most families, part of being a little kid meant that his older siblings picked on him. Gordie, Dan, and Chris were too far removed in age from Goose to worry about scrapping with him, but Rob was only four years older. That left Goose with a target on his back.

"The one who beat me up most was Rob," he confessed. "But I figured out a secret move I called the Treatment. I'd take my fists and stick them into the sides of his neck so it would sort of tickle and hurt at the same time. He'd start laughing and lose control."

Like millions of Americans, he watches his brother compete against the world's best athletes every weekend. A sliver of pride creeps into Goose's voice, knowing that he got the better of Rob. Not many others do.

"That's the only way he wouldn't be able to beat me up, when I gave him the Treatment. It's funny when I do it to him."

"It puts your whole body numb," Rob explained. "It's hard to get out of. But it's always cheap. He does it when I'm not looking. That's the only reason it works."

Once he attended high school, it was expected that Goose would shine on the field where his brothers had starred. He landed a spot on the varsity team as a sophomore receiver, where the team posted an 0-9 record. Yet he kept plugging away. By his senior season, the statistics were impressive: fifty-three receptions, 762 yards, and eleven touchdowns. He also played safety, compiling forty-three tackles, eight interceptions (one for a touchdown), and two fumble recoveries. And as an added bonus, he punted, with an average of 35.4 yards, and kicked extra points.

At Williamsville North, he broke career records in receptions, yards, and touchdowns. Considering his brothers' accomplishments, this is no small feat.

"He was physically a little smaller than his brothers at that age," Mammoliti, his high school coach, recalled. "But he got taller, more physical. He has superior hands and eyes. His ability to jump is the thing that really stands out. He never let the ball come to him. He always went up to the ball. We have shots of him where he's head and shoulders above everyone, grabbing the ball at its highest point. The back-shoulder fade was a big play for us. When we threw it to him, we knew he would go up and get it every time."

Gordy is proud of his son, because at first it did not appear that Goose was committed to training. When he reached eighth grade, he wavered. Some days he worked out; others he skipped. His father kept prodding, but his efforts were not making a difference.

"I was always on him," Gordy recalled. "I'd say, you gonna lift today? Did you do it already? Do you even care? If you don't, fine, but quit wasting my time."

Gordy phoned his oldest son, playing minor-league baseball, and asked for assistance.

"I told Gordie I needed some help with his brother. I tried to motivate him but it just wasn't working anymore. That's when Gord put out a challenge. Thankfully, Goose responded, because I didn't know what else to do."

Despite the ten-year age difference, there is a special bond between Gordie and Goose.

"Gord was my favorite brother growing up," Goose said. "He's really good with kids. He always had time for me, and when we fought, it was always just joking around. He challenged me that whoever worked out more would get a hundred dollars. I had to do my best to keep up with him."

The push from Gordie made a difference.

"Once his older brother challenged him, I saw his talents start to come out," Gordy said. "He showed drive and focus. There was no stopping him. You've either got it or you don't, and he's got it now."

Nearly thirty colleges sent recruitment letters to Goose asking him to consider playing football at their school, including several big-name and Ivy League schools. Despite his impressive high school stats, only the University at Buffalo and Kansas State offered scholarships.

"I would have liked to go to Boston College to be close to Rob," he said. "A lot of MAC [Mid-American Conference] schools were looking at me, but I didn't get any offers. The Ivy League schools don't offer scholarships. So it was UB or Kansas State."

The formula had worked for his brothers, so Goose decided to follow the family footsteps, traveling out of state. Gordy believes this was a wise move.

"I wanted my kids to go away," he said. "I pushed for it. I went away to Syracuse, and it was the best learning experience, living on your own. You find out about yourself. If the boys went to UB, they would have been back at the house all the time. Not to say that's a bad thing, but if you go away, you learn to grow up and live on your own and depend on yourself. You don't need Mom and Dad anymore. You come out with new friends and you know how to act. You can survive in the real world instead of being coddled by your parents. My kids aren't scared of anything. They're not missing home. They know how easy it is to make new friends. I told Goose, if you want to go to UB, that's fine. It would make things a hell of a lot easier on me. But I think you'd be better off down the road to move on."

The key to a successful pattern of kids moving away often lies in the oldest child, and Gordie's achievements in Jacksonville inspired the others.

"If Gordie had a bad time, things might have been different," their father mused. "He had such a great experience when he went away. All the other boys lived off that experience. Danny went down to visit his brother and realized you can do all kinds of stuff. Mom and Dad aren't here to yell at you. The boys needed to experiment on their own but stay away from drugs and do the right stuff. You can have fun and still do the right thing. Now that's what Goose is going to do."

"Goose is very intelligent," his father reflected. "He's more quiet than some of the others. He'll shake your hand and look you in the eyes, but he doesn't go out of his way. During the time between high school and Kansas State, I wanted him to work sales on the floor at G&G. He could have made decent money and learned how to sell, but he wasn't ready to deal with people. He wasn't there yet, and that's fine too."

Instead, Goose stocked shelves and spent time working out in his basement, following the rigorous training schedule sent to him by Kansas State's football program. He hung out with friends, surfed the Net, and followed the exploits of his three NFL brothers. Without prompting, he could recite Rob's up-to-date stats on any given week.

When they were kids, Gordy coached the other boys in baseball and hockey. As they grew older, he began to phase out of that. Work took up much of his time. But Goose was left out of the tradition.

"He had good grades in school," Gordy said, "so I asked him what he wanted for a gift."

"All I want is for you to coach my team," Goose answered.

Gordy could not muster the heart to turn down such a personal request.

"As much as I wanted to get away from coaching, I never

could," he admitted. "I coached Goose in baseball. He's a great player, always the best athlete, and a team leader. For a long time he led by performance. He wasn't the type to huddle people up and say, 'Let's go.' But near the end, when other kids moped around, he'd get in their face and tell them to grow up. And that's just what he did. He needed a little jump start, but he's grown up more and more."

For now, Goose represents the future, the brimming potential of the Gronkowski family. *There is another one coming . . .* He may outshine them, or prove an exclamation point to their successes. Yet in 2012 there was a tangible sense that Goose's story had yet to be written.

Gordie believes his littlest brother could become the best athlete of the five.

"He's going to Kansas State, a Division One school, on a full scholarship, and then maybe going pro. I'll probably have four brothers playing in the NFL. It's the coolest feeling in the world."

The brothers line up on a couch in their Amherst, New York, family room.
From left, Rob, Dan, Goose, Gordie, Chris.

In Los Angeles for the ESPY Awards during summer 2012, hamming it up on
the red carpet. From left, Gordy, Dan, Gordie, Rob, and Chris.

13

Get Gronked!

"Grinding no matter what the situation is. Now get hyped and get Gronked! Whoo!"

— ROB GRONKOWSKI

HAVING COACHED FOUR GRONKOWSKI brothers throughout their high school football careers — three of whom made it to the NFL and the fourth bound for a major college program — Mike Mammoliti has often been asked how he managed to keep their egos in check. The answer is simple.

"There were no egos," he said. "They weren't those kind of kids. Mom and Dad would never let them be that way. I never saw them walk around school and say, 'Look at me.' They never talked down to people. Never. They joked around with me, but never out of meanness. They were pretty humble kids."

With Rob a featured performer in the Super Bowl, Mammoliti fielded calls from national outlets like the *Boston Globe* and the *Washington Post*. Reporters looked for some nugget to expose, some dark secret about Rob that might earn them a front-page scoop. Mammoliti had no such stories to share.

"All the Gronkowskis are really bright kids. They all had averages of ninety-two or above. Sometimes you look at them and think, wow! The big-dumb-jock stereotype just doesn't hold true with these guys. Mom and Dad made sure of that. It's a credit to them."

On a weekend in early March, 2012, with the sun shining and temperatures climbing toward the sixties, the Gronkowski family home in Amherst was overrun with cars. Seven vehicles spread across the driveway, two SUVs splayed at angles near the garage door. License plates from four states were represented. Gordie, Chris, and Rob were all home for the weekend.

Inside, the spacious house had morphed to a grown-up man cave. Empty juice glasses littered the kitchen table. On the counter, a blender jar was open, a large plastic bin of protein powder uncapped. Chris stood nearby, pouring a mixed concoction into a mug. Early Sunday morning, the boys and their father walked the floor wearing T-shirts, socks, and sweatpants.

"There's no question I'm not making it to work on time," Gordie told no one in particular when his father stepped from the room. "I'm just putting that out there. I hope Pops doesn't mind."

The home was a neighborhood gathering place. From the basement came primal shouts, sporadic grunts, and calls of "Let's go!" Friends congregated near the weight benches, working out to an Insanity DVD.

"Sounds like somebody's getting pumped up," Chris said with a laugh.

Rob hobbled past on crutches, knee bent to avoid putting weight on his ankle. Protected by a two-piece cast, he was only weeks removed from surgery. His father detailed the procedure, explaining that it was not career-threatening.

"You don't hear of players retiring because of a bad ankle," Gordy said. "A knee, yes, but not an ankle. Once it heals, it will actually be better. Wire was wrapped around the stretched tendons, which pull the tendons back together so they'll heal strong. In the past, doctors would put two screws in from either side and six weeks later take them out. Hopefully that would hold things in place. Now the wires wrap around it and stay in there forever. If he ever hurts that again, it will be very difficult to get that wire apart."

Although classified as minor surgery, the procedure took nearly three hours. Recovery is expected to last ten weeks. Rob was confident he would be ready to go when Patriots' training camp began in August.

Plans were underway for a busy off-season. While Rob and Chris continued to heal, Dan spent time in Florida, training so he could make an impact with the Browns in the fall. He also landed a bit part in a movie starring Mark Wahlberg.

The rest of the clan scheduled a trip to Hollywood for NFL Network interviews, photo shoots with various magazines, and even discussions about a reality TV show.

While they see themselves as a regular family from Buffalo, with five rough-and-tumble boys, the Gronks have turned into a national phenomenon. Everyone, it seemed, wanted a piece of the Gronkowskis.

"This doesn't stop," Gordy said. "Every single day something comes up."

As the patriarch, Gordy wants to manage this growing empire and maximize his sons' successes. At the same time, he walks a fine line, remaining cautious so the bombarding offers do not consume his family.

"We've got a product that people want," he reflected. "But you have to watch out for the sharks. They're all over right now, take my word. Everyone is trying to get something. I've encountered people who talk well, promise the world, drop a hundred freaking names, but they're useless. We're trying to keep it balanced, because there is a lot going on right now."

Even before the incident at Boston's TD Garden, Gordy saw firsthand how popular Rob was in the week leading up to the Super Bowl. On the streets of Indianapolis, after leaving an evening event, the Gronkowski brothers waited on a sidewalk while Chris left to get his car. People noticed Rob and pushed toward him, seeking his attention, asking for autographs.

"The whole street went crazy," Gordy said. "We had to run into a bank where security guards locked doors and shut all the shades while we waited for Chris to pull up and get us. We had to hustle Rob into the car. He's a big celebrity wherever he goes."

One reason for the exploding popularity, Gordy believes, is that in addition to Rob's on-field success, he retains an air of silliness. He is still just a big kid enjoying each day. He's not above poking fun at himself or others, a trait shared by all the brothers.

An example was Rob's very public lobbying to be on the cover of the video game *Madden 13*. He took to the airwaves and asked fans to vote for him, even making a home video with his brothers and posting it on YouTube.

Sitting on a couch, his casted ankle elevated, Rob wears shorts and a white T-shirt with sunglasses perched on the crown of his head. With a metal crutch across his lap, Rob looks into the camera and makes an impassioned plea.

"What's up, Gronk Nation fans? I'm going to tell you why I should be voted for the cover of *Madden 13* this year."

Goose, wearing vintage '90s-style Zubaz pants, stands before Rob. On command, he pushes down on the crutch, providing resistance while Rob executes several curls to show his dedication to working out. The camera pans right, where Chris does push-ups and Gordie, next to him on the floor, performs sit-ups, using a loaf of bread as a substitute medicine ball. Both of them wear Zubaz pants as well.

When the camera swings back to Rob, he twitches and jerks his head so that his sunglasses drop to the bridge of his nose.

"Grinding no matter what the situation is," he intones. "Now get hyped and get Gronked! Whoo!"

Their father smiled and shook his head when discussing the video.

"Rob was a goofball about the cover of *Madden* and people loved it," he said. "Everybody is so serious, but those knuckleheads threw that thing together. People love their personalities. They can be prim and proper when they need to be, but they're out there having fun. They're just enjoying life."

The individual traits are evident to anyone who meets the brothers.

"Their personalities are all a little different," said Drew Rosen-haus, the agent who represents Dan, Chris, and Rob. "Rob has a great personality. Dan is more serious, more mature. It might have to do with the fact that he's the older brother. Chris is the most intense of the three. I've met Gordie, the oldest brother, and he's a fun guy. It will be fun to see how the youngest, Glenn, develops. Each of these guys is special in their own way."

Glenn Gronkowski, Gordy's brother, has seen his nephews grow from boys to men.

"I can't say anything bad about them," he said. "They're good kids. They have their priorities straight and that's the important thing. I don't want to pick on other people, but they aren't all tat-tooed up. They don't have bling or jewelry, expensive watches or racecars. They're really grounded young men."

Brittany Gronkowski, Dan's wife, ponders the moment nearly ten years earlier when she saw the Gronkowski clan for the first time. As a high school senior, she attended the funeral of a fam-ily friend on a snowy February day in Buffalo. The Gronkowskis were there as well.

"I saw all these big guys standing near a black conversion van," she recalled. "There was a small car, like a Toyota Corolla, parked behind them."

At the cemetery, cars clustered close to the grave. The van was blocked in, but the owner wanted to leave.

"Their dad and all the brothers surrounded the car, leaned down and counted, one, two, three," Brittany said. "They picked it up and moved it a few feet, then set it down. They all got in the van and drove away. I rubbed my eyes. Did that just happen? Now that I know them, it makes sense. But at the time, I thought, who are these people?"

Shortly after that, she visited the Gronkowski house, with a hint of trepidation. Brittany was not sure what to expect. Teens gathered in the spacious basement. She enjoyed talking with Dan. She was struck by his courtesy, drawn to someone the same age. The younger brothers, however, recognized a pretty girl and vied for her attention.

"Rob and Chris were showing me their oblique muscles," she recalled. "I thought those guys were weird. They were asking, 'Do girls like this muscle? We've heard girls like muscles.'" Brittany laughs at the memory of a stereotypical annoying little brother. "Bear in mind that at the time, Rob was in eighth grade."

"It really didn't hit me how special these athletes were until Dan and Chris were playing together at Maryland," Mammoliti said. "I had gone with friends to a sports bar. We were having dinner and somebody put the game on. I was standing there and watched them in the same package on the goal line. I jumped up and yelled, 'Hey, those are my guys!'"

As their high school coach, Mammoliti is humbled to say he had some contribution to the development of the brothers. He's thrilled at their successes on the field. Yet he's also glad that the Gronkowskis are such good people.

"You would be hard-pressed to find five brothers like this," Mammoliti said. "They are always positive about each other. Sure, they kid and bust each other's chops, but these guys have each other's backs and they have from the first day I met them. It's a really cool thing to see how close they are."

Longtime family friend Chris Heim played football with both Rob and Chris when they were kids. In fact, a scar on his arm is a permanent reminder of the time he and Chris blocked a kick in a high school game.

"I've known Rob since fifth grade," Heim said. "He and his brothers are good people to be around. When they made it to the league, they didn't change. They're still the same people they've always been."

Success in any endeavor is a result of hard work. Each of the Gronkowskis displays drive and dedication, but with the added advantage of family support. Every brother has fed off another brother's success. They encourage and push one another, striving toward the next level. This is evident in their game-day rituals. A few hours before kickoff, messages between brothers and their father zing back and forth through cyberspace.

"Remember how hard you worked to get here," Gordy texts Dan.

"Get hyped and get focused," Gordie texts Rob.

"I had a better workout than you," Chris texts Dan and Rob. "But have a good game anyway."

The messages are meant to amuse but also to reinforce the strength of their family bond.

"It's a little motivation," Dan explained. "It helps you focus, knowing you've got the support of your brothers and family."

Still, the Gronkowskis recognize that careers in professional sports can be fleeting. There is a fine line between making a team and being cut. Injuries are only one play away.

Five boys, five star athletes. It is too early in their careers to call it a dynasty, but the Gronkowskis' success is remarkable, the type of alignment that occurs rarely, once a generation. Sometimes, raised expectations can lead to a quick flameout, or a resentment of the bright lights and media attention.

But by staying true to their values and placing emphasis on family first, that doesn't appear to be an issue for any of the boys. They are smart, tough, and grounded, focusing on new goals. Get in a good workout, have a great practice, win the game. When the wins pile up, success follows.

So what matters is not the stardom that seems so prominent now. That will be temporary, however long it lasts. What matters is that the family unit is tight. Whenever the attention fades — be it next year, in two years, or a decade from now — the family will remain connected by passion, dedication, and a love of the competition and experiences they have shared, growing up Gronk.

Foxborough, on a bright autumn Sunday. Under the watchful eyes of thousands of screaming Patriots' fans, a football is booted into a high arc. Giant men charge down the field, colliding into each other with abandon, pushing, clutching, lunging to make a tackle. As the whistle blows, players disentangle and head for the sidelines.

Trotting onto the field is quarterback Tom Brady, with steel in his eyes. Ten other offensive players jog toward the huddle, including big No. 87. Rob Gronkowski, with twin black streaks smudged across his cheeks, leans down to hear the call. On cue, everyone claps and shuffles to the line of scrimmage. The center wraps his huge hand around the ball, checking the defensive scheme. Brady squats behind him, barking orders.

On the far end of the line, Rob puts his hand on the ground and runs through a series of progressions. Excitement courses through him. Background noise dissolves until all he hears is Brady's curt cadence. Rob can't wait for the snap, can't wait to spring forward and collide with a linebacker, then shake loose and sprint across the middle of the field. Playing football has defined his life since eighth grade. Without thinking, a smile crosses his lips.

Scattered across the country, like millions of fans, Rob's brothers, his mom, and their friends are tuned into television sets, watching to see what he will do.

In an instant, the ball is snapped.

In the stands, Gordy sits anxiously, pushing sunglasses against the bridge of his nose. He watches with arms folded, chest high with pride. That is one of his sons, a star tight end in the National Football League.

Acknowledgments

Thanks to my friend Hans Kullerkupp, who suggested this project. Thanks also to my great editors, Susan Ballard and Wynne Everett, and people who contributed their talents to help develop this book, including Mark Pogodzinski (www.nofrillsbuffalo.com), Alex Turnwall (www.hifinit.com), Stuart Shapiro, Jay Mandel, and Susan Canavan. I appreciate everyone who gave their time to be interviewed.

I owe so much to my dad, Tom, my late mother, Mary Jo, and Teri Miranda. I love them all.

While my first choice is to see the Buffalo Bills win a Super Bowl, the next best thing would be for all the Gronkowski boys to win one as well.
— Jeff Schober

I'm so proud of my five sons. Not only are they great athletes, but they're also great young gentlemen. Thanks to my mom and dad for putting me on this earth and to my brother, Glenn, for showing me the right direction. Frank Viggato, my high school baseball coach, always believed in me. Thanks to coaches Frank Maloney and Jerry Angelo for giving me the last scholarship. I also want to thank Diane for giving birth and helping me raise five wonderful boys.

— Gordy Gronkowski